About Mai Ghoussoub

'Mai lived to fight the Lebanese civil war, and she was living and thinking in the heart of the project that is Lebanon's only hope of liberation – by establishing a unified civil identity beyond sects; a unified civil culture beyond linguistic and ethnic boundaries, East or West.'
Adonis

'Seeing her around Beirut or London was like catching sight of Debbie Harry in New York. She was an icon, she made things happen.'
Daily Star

'She was open to the future because she was naturally, independently and continuously creative. Few countries need these qualities as much as Lebanon. I hope a new generation will step forward to try and fill her role with the same intelligence and humanity.'
Anthony Barnett, *OpenDemocracy*

'Her life is almost a continuous expression in her sculptures, installations, performances and writings, and her travels and her relationships. Her overwhelming sensitivity and her energy spread without fragmenting. Mai, who was at once very patriotic, was at the same time a woman of the world ... she was being herself without any compromise, but she always cared for everyone.'
Abbas Beydoun

'She was a pioneer in establishing freedom of expression, and being open to all other cultures.'   Rawas

'According to Ghoussoub, resentment is a feeling that every human has, but being civilised will restrict this feeling of resentment, and she doesn't consider punishment as revenge, because revenge makes punishment barbaric.'   Mikhael al Khouri, *al-Nahar*

'For Mai, all aspects of art – music, sculpture, dance, literature – were elements of a continuum, and she made no intellectual difference between them. She did, however, see sculpture as her work – but writing was a compulsion and an urge, an avocation that often took her unaware and tore into time that was always too little and too full.'   Aamer Hussein

'The impact of war on human behaviour – in all its tragedy and irony – was a formative preoccupation for Ghoussoub. One can only regret that her lucid voice has been so prematurely silenced.' *New Statesman*

'A formidable woman, a fine artist, and an inspired publisher.'   PEN

Mai Ghoussoub

SELECTED WRITINGS

Edited by
Rebecca O'Connor

SAQI

London San Francisco Beirut

ISBN: 978-0-86356-642-4

First published by Saqi, 2008

A full CIP record for this book is available from the British Library.
A full CIP record for this book is available from the Library of Congress.

Manufactured in Lebanon

SAQI

26 Westbourne Grove, London W2 5RH
825 Page Street, Suite 203, Berkeley, California 94710
Tabet Building, Mneimneh Street, Hamra, Beirut
www.saqibooks.com

Contents

Acknowledgments

Thanks to the following publications, in which some of these essays and stories have appeared: 111101 Project, *The Cuirt Annual, Divas, al-Hayat, Hikayat: Short Stories by Lebanese Women, Imagined Masculinities, Al Jadid, Lebanon, Lebanon*, openDemocracy, and *The Predicament of the Individual in the Middle East*.

Special thanks also to Spencer Platt for permission to reprint his photograph in 'Beirut and Contradiction'.

To the Lady at the Counter of the Museum Shop

The Lady at the Counter
The Museum Shop
Mauritshuis
The Hague

Dear Madam

I visited the museum shop with my sister yesterday at around 2 p.m. and we bought a few items, among them two pairs of pearl earrings (like the ones in the Vermeer painting). Something very strange and funny happened. You brought out two pairs of earrings and one of them disappeared. We looked everywhere, but they seemed to have evaporated! So you brought out a third pair, and we left having bought two pairs. But the mystery remained unsolved.

We travelled by train to our hotel in Amsterdam in order to catch a plane to London. While removing my coat on the train a young man approached me, saying something had fallen from it. I looked on the floor and what did I see but the pair of earrings that had disappeared! They must have stuck to the lining or a buttonhole, or somewhere none of us had seen. By then it was too late to return to the museum. My sister and I were really surprised, for we had walked all the way from the museum to the train and the earrings could have dropped anywhere along the way and we would all have continued to puzzle over the mystery of the 'evaporated' earrings.

I have visited the Mauritshuis, and your shop, many times. I often sit for a long time in front of *The Girl with a Pearl Earring*. My first reaction was to say to myself that as soon as I returned to London I'd post the earrings back to you. But my sister said that I should keep this pair, because this pair stuck to me in the most unbelievable way. So I've decided instead to send payment.

Please charge my credit card for the amount of 18 something Euros (I don't remember the exact price). It is between 18 and 19 Euros.

I thought I'd tell you the story and not just send the payment because I still find it strange and funny myself.

Yours sincerely

M. Ghoussoub

Beirut: A Visible City on the Road

Last week I was sitting through a four-hour train ride from Liverpool to London. In the seats behind me were two young men, one Asian and one West African, both in their early twenties.

They had with them a little gadget broadcasting a very funny Asian sitcom, *Goodness Gracious Me*. I could hear the sketches very clearly, to the point where I decided to put down the book I was reading and listen. Soon I was really enjoying what I was hearing and had forgotten all about my book. Suddenly, from a few seats ahead, came a man in his thirties – big, white, very white, almost pink – with a shaved head and a big tattoo covering most of his right shoulder. He started screaming and insulting the two young men.

'Put that down. Understand me?'

I could see a fight brewing.

But to my surprise, the two young men complied immediately. I felt ashamed of myself; I should have intervened. I was offended for them. I was aggressed by the man's rudeness, and I was in no doubt that racism had something to do with his atrocious behaviour. I am telling this story because I still feel ashamed for keeping quiet. I could at least have told him to ask politely, I could have come to the rescue of these two kids by saying that I was enjoying the sketches too. I didn't, because my space of thinking and acting was restricted by the carriage space. I still feel bad, because I might have been the only one who could have intervened: I understood both the desire of this pink man to defend his individual space and the need of the two young men to share theirs. I am, after all, whatever changes I have witnessed in my life, still from a city, Beirut, a city *par excellence* and moreover a city located on the shores of the Mediterranean, this space/mood that has always known how to include 'the other' and turn it into a 'self'.

I say a city *par excellence* because 'a city is a social community, because it organises itself in a space that assembles its members, because it is inscribed in time and in this sense it is not static even in awareness and representation, because it is made of tensions and divergences, of interactions, of conflicts between its actors.' But a city on the shores of a shared sea is so different from my train carriage, for when things become impossible on land one can always look out, breathe the sea air; the sea opens up to let its inhabitants sail away, or at least dream of reaching other shores.

Beirut! Yes, so different from this train carriage, but somehow similar because of the number of languages that were reaching my ears from the other seats. Beirut – which I have never wanted to become an obsession, which carries with it the lies that are the essence of nostalgia – is still for me what Venice represented to Marco Polo. Allow me to borrow shamelessly from Italo Calvino's wonderful *Invisible Cities*:

> 'Sir,' says Marco Polo to Kublai Khan, 'now I have told you about the cities I know.'
>
> 'There is still one city of which you never speak.'
>
> Marco Polo bowed his head.
>
> 'Venice,' the Khan said.

Marco smiled: 'What else do you think I have been telling you about?'

The emperor did not turn a hair. 'And yet I have never heard you mention that name.'

And Polo said, 'Every time I describe a city I am saying something about Venice.'

This is why, every time I describe a city, or visit one, I am describing Beirut and revisiting it.

This is not an homage, not a celebration of a city; far from it. For, unfortunately, I also owe this city for familiarising me with the injustices and corruption that one encounters, to a greater or lesser degree, throughout the cities of the world. Let's call it a *recognition*, a fact that I did not appreciate enough when I first settled in London, away from the Mediterranean, that open promise that had gently caressed my adolescence before throwing me, through fire and blood, from its shores. It threw me towards a city polar opposite to the one I grew up in, an Anglo-Saxon city to the core, a city that lived inside, in dim light, with no shore and no café life. Beirut is a city *al fresco*, very conspicuous thanks to its loud fun, to its noisy joys, but also to the thunderous rumblings of its violent outbreaks. My lucidity is unfortunately indebted to these opposing worlds. Without Beirut, the city of the south, without its life in translation, I would never have been capable of surviving happily in the cities of the north. It is thanks to my background that I felt that my duty was not only to integrate positively into another urban space, but also and mainly to feel unashamed about dreaming of influencing, of making an impact on 'the other', on the shifting identities of 'the desirable' urban spaces, the metropolises of today.

Background! I love this word, so much more desirable than the word 'identity', or 'root'. Identity and root presume a settled or pure essence; they thrive in times of trouble, often preceding them. Background is synonymous with base, it is located somewhere *behind*, a reality one can refer to, but which can be ignored or abandoned. Our background is not exactly our root; it is the soil in which many realities can grow, but where others can be planted as well.

'A carrot is a root,' says my friend to her husband, who keeps nagging her about returning to his country, to his roots. 'I am not a carrot!' she keeps screaming back at him.

Beirut was, is, a city that travels in many directions. Let's look at its calligraphy: it moves and reads in many directions, right to left, left to right, and, yes, for a long time now from top to bottom or bottom to top. I am speaking of the multitude of signs and adverts and billboard invitations to consume that coloured my trips to school for many years and that still fascinate me whenever I walk the city. When you read in opposite directions you're not impermeable to other readings. Maybe this is why, when, during the civil war, my colleague André Gaspard and I landed in Britain, knowing almost nobody here, we felt unselfconscious about the difficulties of starting a bookshop and publishing house, and functioning in what was our third language, English.

I'll tell you an embarrassing story: when we opened our bookshop we needed addresses for our catalogue mailing list. This was 1979; we were newly arrived in England. We went through the telephone directory for nights on end looking for potential customers, through the listings, looking for the al-something, or the Oriental this or that ... I'm afraid many of our catalogues may have landed in Chinese restaurants or Thai sex shops.

We were a bit lost, but no doubt keen. I sometimes think that this naïve optimism is inherited from my great-grandfather, who, fleeing another war, the first big one, jumped on a boat, paying the fee to the captain to take him to America. The captain threw my great-grandfather, as well as many of his co-villagers, onto the shores of French Guinea. 'You are in America,' he said to them. This is why they called Africa 'America' in my grandfather's village for years afterwards. Meanwhile in Africa, my great-grandfather made a decent living and sent home money to educate his children, who acquired, hopefully, a better knowledge of geography.

If I hadn't been brought up in a city that wrote in opposite directions I wouldn't have been able to survive and enjoy the London of today, with its multi-ethnic fusion culture and juxtaposed realities. Beirut, with its words moving in different directions, made me sceptical, very early on, of the word 'truth', and of the now-unfortunately fashionable labels of 'evil' and 'good'. It was in my *Lycée Français de Beirut* that the Crusaders were either saints or cruel colonisers, depending on whether the textbooks were in French, from left to right, or in Arabic, from right to left. These opposite but coexistent readings warned me that truth can be perceived differently according to one's location in terms of history, geography and, most importantly, aspiration. This is why I found myself sitting on the train refusing to accept this little fight over space as a so-called 'clash of cultures' or worse, a 'clash of civilisations'.

But it was also because in Beirut I had read Simone de Beauvoir in French, Abu Nuwas in Arabic and Margaret Mead at the American University of Beirut, that I could face this old male chauvinist English banker who kept asking for my boss when I came to open an account for Saqi Books. This was a long time ago – some twenty-five years back – and male chauvinism has witnessed a few defeats since then in Britain. But this dignified-looking, tweed-jacketed man didn't find it at all undignified to keep asking me, as if he was hard of hearing, to 'let your boss come and sign for the account'. And I kept telling him, 'But I am also a director,' what he called 'a boss', but to no avail. I moved from his bank to another without wasting much time, and lived happily ever after.

It is because I walked from Achrafieh to Ras Beirut, via Ain al-Rumaneh or al-Bourj, by houses that offered their modest balconies to my eyes or their imposing high-rise glass façades, as well as their Oriental late-Ottoman arcades, that I feel at home in New York as well as in Fez. I walked the same route all through my early twenties, humming the tunes of Edith Piaf, Um Kulsum and Feyrouz, as well as John Coltrane and the Rolling Stones, so that when I reached other cities, *any* other city, I could sing and dance to the same rhythms of their inhabitants.

I went to another city, and it became mine, I became proud of some of its monuments and customs: London is home as well. London, so different, but also a space that generously lives out its coexisting realities today. Let me quote from *Invisible Cities* once more:

'In Mauralia,' says Marco Polo to Kublai Khan, 'the traveller is invited to visit the city and at the same time, to examine some old postcards that show it as it used to be: The same identical square with a hen in the place of the bus station, a bandstand in the place of the overpass, two young ladies with a parasol in the place of the munitions factory. If the traveller does not wish to disappoint the inhabitants he must praise the postcard city and prefer it to the present one ... It is pointless to ask whether the new ones (cities) are better than the old, since there is no connection between them, just as the old postcards do not depict Mauralia as it was, but a different city which, by chance, was called Mauralia, like this one.'

I hope I did not describe my city as it is portrayed in the postcards, for I am not one for nostalgia, and I thank Beirut for having prepared me to see migration as a promise of adventure. I have to say that only London – the London of today, not that of Victorian postcards – has given me the chance to live in a multiracial environment, where the Asian is the computer engineer who connects me to the net, as well as the newsagent next door or the student in my evening class, while my other city, Beirut today, gives me one image, a unique and narrow one of an Asian: an oppressed, over-exploited immigrant housemaid.

Let me tell you about my latest experience in London. Over the last three years I've been exploring the theme of prejudice through appearance and dress code. In *Dressing – Readdressing,* an installation

that dressed people on book covers or cinema posters in the outfits of 'the other', I have been observing the reaction of 'locals' to the shift in external appearance. In London and Vancouver, the symbols were 'orientalised', while in Beirut they were 'occidentalised'.

A few months ago I pushed the exploration further: I dressed as a veiled Lolita, sucking the pipe of a narghile instead of a lollipop; I wore the long robe of Lawrence of Arabia; and a Muslim woman's white tennis outfit, covering my whole body except for my eyes. The latter outfit was purchased in Egypt, in an Islamic sports shop for women. I walked the streets of east London in all of these costumes, carrying my tennis racquet, or sucking my lollipop through my veil, and waited to see how people would respond. Nothing: the Londoners turned their gaze immediately away! They didn't see me! They didn't interfere! They saw but made sure they hadn't stared. I admit that I am still puzzled by this over-tolerant attitude. If I had done the same in Paris, I would have at least heard the familiar *'Rentrez chez vous!'* In Beirut, I am sure, a crowd of kids would have pointed their fingers at me and most probably followed me around.

I hope that soon I'll take my performance and my artistic exploration of 'prejudice' to as many cities as possible.

I hope my city, Beirut, is relearning to be a true cosmopolitan space, a cosmopolitan space in the age of global reality, where the 'others' are, again, also 'us' and where juxtaposition is fighting hierarchy.

Once more from Calvino before I go:

The question that now begins to gnaw at your mind is more anguished: outside Penthesilia does an outside exist? Or, no matter how far you go from the city, will you only pass from one limbo to another, never managing to leave it?

M in Exile

M had always dreamt of travels, change and new beginnings. This was before M was forced to leave her country. Exile did not seem like the worst nightmare. Suffocating under terrible conditions in her 'own' country seemed worse than anything.

For M, exile was a step that should have meant a new life. She was positive about it. She would learn a new language, learn new habits, and gain more freedom of movement as a woman than she had done in her own country.

But exile means newcomers and hosts, and the hosts haven't had the same experience; they haven't experienced bloodthirsty dictatorships for more than a century. The hosts have long forgotten about the realities of civil war. The hosts don't feel the urge to adapt to her ways.

She had to adapt and she did it pretty well. But her father felt diminished in exile. His values were still deeply rooted in his country: honour, respect within the community, bread-winning for his family. He found it very difficult to adapt to a situation where he was 'just nothing', not even saluted by the shopkeeper on his way to work. Her mother, if she missed her country, didn't show it, for all she wanted was to make sure that her children found happiness wherever they were.

M's country is normal now. M believed that going back would bring happiness: her parents, like all those who have lost something, were constantly nostalgic for all the 'wonderful things back home'. Nostalgia always works this way: you remember happy things and obliterate all that was ugly, frustrating and difficult in what is lost or missing.

So M went back home as soon as the situation permitted. She was full of hope. But home was not exactly home. She had another home she had occupied for many years now; M had lived her adolescence away from her country, from its language, its streets and habits. Only the food was familiar: her mother kept cooking it at home.

There were two Ms.

M1 loved it back home; she found things the way she had left them when she was a child and lived happily ever after among 'her people'.

M2 felt a foreigner in her country, for she grew up with different habits, made friends in exile. Now she dressed and spoke and looked like 'a foreigner' in this recovered context. Home was no longer exactly home.

Is there one home for an exiled person after many years of 'being an exile'?

Why should we have one home in today's world?

M1 wanted to start from where she began.

M2 realised that there was no going back.

They Are Telling Us

They are telling us our lives are five times more valuable than yours and your families', your friends' lives. They are telling us we shall destroy every corner of your cities, every little café you ever sat in, every good memory of your fun-loving country. Those of you who inherited a memory of suffering don't feel anything for the suffering of others.

Abu Ghraib

All I can do is scream through my keyboard.

Do the soldiers torturers act with such abject cruelty out of racism? Racism is not enough to explain their behaviour, their abuse, the joy on their faces while they are attacking the prisoners in their flesh and their dignity.

Are they aware that the only justification left to their leaders was to save the poor Iraqi people from a regime that behaved incessantly like they do in these pictures that make me want to throw up? Have they studied Saddam's methods of abuse and, assured of their efficiency, felt they should re-enact them? Keeping prisoners naked, sodomising them or obliging them to have sex with each other, were common practice in Saddam's jails, in Abu Ghraib in particular. Dragging someone like you would drag an abused dog is the ultimate humiliation for an Arab man: dogs are *najes* in Islamic tradition, synonymous with dirt.

Are they aware, were they ever told, that those who behaved similarly in Bosnia are being tried for war crimes in The Hague?

Depraved people like to abuse and torture, but there are too many of them here to allow us to speak of psychologically deranged individuals. They are too many and they are seemingly not hiding from their fellow-soldiers and the rest of the prison guards. They are even taking souvenir snapshots, like hunters who smile for the camera, proudly holding their trophy prey.

How can this be? Can we ever say 'never again' with any conviction? We have asked these questions before. We have heard the same justifications before: 'We did not know!' or: 'We were obeying orders!' Now there is a new phrase: 'We were investigating the claims (for months).'

The family of a woman soldier shown abusing prisoners has released a picture of her tenderly holding a young Iraqi child. It is meant to show that she is a loving person who cares for the Iraqis. She was told to obey orders, declare her family.

Another familiar story! You may love children, be sweet and caring, but the rules of war are special and they turn you into something particularly ugly. The secrecy of occupying armies turns soldiers into little gods shaping and coercing peoples' bodies. The secrecy of occupying armies has also turned women soldiers into sadistic pornographers.

The leaders were 'investigating the claims'; the soldiers, the guards were obeying orders. But even the doctors who were conducting experiments in Nazi camps were supposedly obeying orders. Can it be the same? They always seem to have obeyed with great enthusiasm.

I feel angry and lost. I do not know where to look for hope. I cannot even repeat in front of people in the country where I come from in the Middle East that in Western democracies people in power are accountable. How can I tell them now that democracy, more than any other system, rests on openness and honesty? Those in power in America and Britain have been mainly trying to suppress evidence; they don't even understand the need to resign immediately in the face of these disgusting crimes, so as to have the decency to admit their failure. If they have succeeded in creating disbelief in me, what effect does their behaviour have on people who were already sceptical about the virtues of democracy and the rule of law – never more badly needed in the Arab world than now?

Who is Serious?

The *Washington Post* sees the roots of the Abu Ghraib torture scandal in a 'corrupted culture' which violated the Geneva Conventions and '[distorted] the rule of law'; Human Rights Watch identifies violations that 'reflect official policy authorized at the highest levels' of government; the International Committee of the Red Cross judges that the mistreatment of Iraqi prisoners was not confined to individual cases but formed part of a systematic pattern.

But Douglas Murray knows better. It's nothing but a nasty joke – 'pulling down a man's trousers for kicks'.

After reading his contribution to the Iraq debate, I felt not only like screaming (a response that Murray dismisses as curious) but a kind of fear. Has the time not long passed for justifications based on degrees of aggression against people's bodies, integrity and rights when they are defenceless in front of those who have power over them?

Douglas Murray is not interested in the moral questions raised by torture. He is still arguing as if we had not seen the leaked pictures of the man dragged with a lead around his neck, the tilted bodies chained on bed frames, the naked prisoner terrorised by the threatening dogs, of those who died under interrogation. If he believes in the democratic crusade that ostensibly inspired this war, he should give a little thought to the fact that humiliation is not what the Iraqi people need to believe in this democracy.

Murray says that we only need to read a book to know that 'in any conflict and on any side people behave badly'. Does he mean that if this happens it should be acceptable, that the decent people on each side should not fight tooth and nail to stop it happening, instead of finding excuses and extenuating circumstances?

If there is one book that should be read nowadays, it is Pierre Vidal-Naquet's *Torture: Cancer of Democracy*.

What is it that Murray finds (his recurrent theme) un-'serious'? The fact that we are disgusted by images showing humans inflicting pain and humiliation on other humans who are unable to defend themselves? The fact that we protest when a war presented in moral terms has as one of its results a degradation that echoes what it was fought to end – the cruelty of a regime that violated people's bodies?

What he trivialises as 'pulling down a man's trousers for kicks', a 'penchant for naked pyramids' and 'a dirty girl's perversions' evades troubling, necessary questions about women and their attitude in a war zone. Who can be so sure about the humanising input of women in the army today? Why do the women in these pictures mix sexuality and power as in the porn movies that circulate mainly among males?

There is something disturbing about Murray's dismissive words for those who are shaken by the images of humans being subjected to cruelty and humiliation.

But there seems more than mere denial in Douglas Murray's casual refusal to see the Abu Ghraib actions as torture, or his mocking quote marks around the word 'scandal'. There seems a failure of moral imagination here that an American conservative like John Hulsman does not share.

In the urge to find vindication in the 'large' outcome of the war he so vigorously champions, can Douglas Murray not stop for a second and ask himself why no army or militia seems immune to the exercise of objectification with 'the other's body' in the context of occupation, incarceration and interrogation? This sad, fearful combination of dehumanisation and intimate physical aggression has been practised too often, by too many, in history. It does not allow anybody to feel civilly superior to anybody else.

Despite this unhappy universality in mankind's behaviour, I believe that we should still give such actions a bad name, and not try to minimise the seriousness of the crime or allow them to go unpunished. This, I believe, is the serious logic of universal, human justice inside the 'scream' that the images of Abu Ghraib provoked in millions of people across the world.

Red Addiction

We were only a dozen from my town to be sent there. *There*. I can still smell the place; I can smell hell creeping inside my nostrils and up to my brain. Every night, a fetid whiff of warm sweat drags me out of bed like a menopausal woman in the midst of sleep. My wife has never understood why I need to take a shower at dawn, a long unending escape under cool water before going back to sleep again. How could she understand? I have never shared my nightmares with her. In our long life together, she has never suspected for a second that it is in her make-up bag always kept in the same place inside the bathroom cabinet that I find peace. It is in the candy-like aroma of her lipsticks that I am freed from the secret that haunts me.

Now that I am too old to protect my secrets, now that my life is regulated by the clock tick-tocking in the dining room, I find it easier to spell out the words stuck persistently in my throat. Now that the stone weighing on my chest, stifling every little pleasure in my life and extinguishing the enjoyment of being has become part of me, I dare speak. I am addicted: only the bright shades of red exposed by the lipsticks in my wife's cabinet keep me going and give me some sense of life and relief. I cannot sleep if I haven't indulged in the brightness of a red lipstick and inhaled its sweet aroma. It is then, and only then, that I can rid myself of the putrid smell of death that has beleaguered my existence.

Every night, for over fifty years now, I lie awake in bed, my eyes wide open in the darkness of our bedroom waiting for stillness to engulf the world before I move silently to the bathroom. I let the water drop heavily into the bathtub and open the cabinet. I take my time, quietly undoing the lid of each lipstick with great care. I take my time bringing the red tube closer to my nose, and I inhale deeply, with my eyes closed. I lean against the wall, eyes still closed, breathing deeply, trying to capture the smell inside my head. I let it seep through every pore of my skin, begging it to invade every bit of awareness left in me. I indulge in deciphering every component of the red scents that permeate my nostrils, getting slowly dizzy with their ethereal tracks until I am appeased.

And when all the lipsticks kept in the bag have gone through this ritual, when their effect has lingered in my head like a sweet warm brandy, I put everything back in exactly the same place; I move slowly towards the shower and stand under it until the strong flow of fresh water splashes out all other sensations. I then go to bed and sink into a dim orange sleep.

Pink Passion, Brun Rose, Flesh Light, Sugar & Spice tubes. Rosewood, Mauve Dream, Devil's Claw, Belle de Jour shades. Pink Promises, Temptation, Heather Mist, Barbarella reds. Haze, Divine, Pepper, Extravagant lipsticks. Light Flash, Xanadu, Pink Ice, Honeypie and Red Mustard pigments.

So many names, so many persistent images.

Maybe I could have told my wife about the origin of my

obsession with her make-up. But I was never able to speak about the war, about the horrors that we discovered in the camp, so how could I tell her about the strange lipstick episode that erupts like a blinding red flash in the midst of my war traumas? I became acquainted with this word 'trauma' through a veteran's magazine when I was still in the army, and before I started painting walls to make a living. White walls, mainly. Nobody ever asked me to paint their walls red.

I was young, not yet twenty years old, when my regiment was assigned to the liberated camp. We had no idea, we didn't know. Even if they had told us before our arrival about the horrific ordeal endured by the inmates, it would have made no difference. It would have been impossible to conceive the scale of the agony if you had not seen it with your own eyes, if you had not smelled it inside your own nostrils. I will never be able to describe its full monstrosity.

I was assigned to the women's ward. Women did not look like women; they were living corpses, in every state of emaciation and disease, lying on bunk beds or on the floor. Some were dead, unnoticed, for they hardly looked that different from the living. No words can convey the frightful scenes we witnessed inside those huts. Our task was to fight death, and death had been the winner for many years in this hideous place called Belsen.

How could anybody have expected that the colour red was going to bring back hope into this hell? But hope came, for a while at least, a very short while; it came like the sudden rise of a bright sun in the middle of a deep dark night. The colour red entered the hut, thanks to the crazy but brilliant initiative of those who had sent a container of lipsticks as a gift: not clothes, blankets or food, as usual and as expected. None of these objects for survival, but a consignment of glittering tubes of glamorous and glowing lipsticks.

Red ripe raisin, delicious good burgundy brew. Autumn terracotta red, the smell of damp earth. Brown clove glaze or ginger flower reds. Cinnamon brick lights and Bordeaux fruity reds.

I don't believe in miracles, but how else can I describe the effect these tubes of scarlet had on these desolate and dying women? They all pulled themselves out of their misery and pains and started sliding the red make-up out of the tubes, looking and selecting, examining, rejecting before picking the right hue.

I remember their eyes; they seem to have invaded their faces and they were, for the first time, focused instead of looking into nowhere. Some women looked like skeletons with those large enquiring eyes, advancing in a disconnected but determined way towards the glittering objects of desire.

They applied it carefully, as if they were fully aware of their gestures, their hands drawing lines like an artist putting the last touches to his or her masterpiece.

Red lips, living lips.

The women were standing, sometimes covered with only a blanket. They smiled and felt and looked womanly. Suddenly they were not just survivors or dying bodies, but women caring for nuances, women revealing their own individual choices, tastes and histories. I realised, full of shame, that I was noticing for the first time their different features. I was ashamed because I had not appreciated that these half-dead women were still clinging to life against all odds; they had protected their dignity, hidden it inside their tortured bodies while their jailers were doing their best to dehumanise them.

Red, just a shade of red, was enough to trigger an affirmation of existence, of the self. They were not just patients and ex-inmates any longer; they were feeling special, they were women conscious of their femininity, ready to face the world with their bright coloured lips.

Red is ruby. Red, a precious gemstone worn in China to promote long life. Red, bold red, the colour of activity and motivation. Reds, sacred and vitalising reds like some hot and rare spices. Red, the colour of fever and its healer.

And then I saw her. She was suddenly standing in the middle of the room. I say she, because I never asked what her name was. I wish I knew her real name. But I was so mesmerised by her appearance that I stood still, paralysed for a very long time. All I could see were her inviting lips, marvellous like a full-bodied wine. I was spellbound, unable to move, oblivious to any other reality but the blazing red emanating from her face. I stood there long after she'd collapsed and they'd carried her away. I could still see her lips when she was no longer there. Later, when it was quiet in the hut, when I started to recover from my numbness and joined the other soldiers, I did not inquire after her name. She died with a smile on her lips, the soldier from the infirmary told us. I felt so guilty and ashamed, for I could not shake the image of her lips from my mind, even after her death. I cannot recall her face; she was all lips, victorious screaming lips over her sunken eyes and bony famished face. 'Ruby' was the name that came naturally to me each time I closed my eyes and thought about her. There hasn't been a day in my life free of Ruby's startling red lips, not a day without the emergence of morbidity into every lively colour my eyes meet.

Maybe I should have told my wife, but it's too late now. I should have told her when I fell in love with her, or, to be more honest, when I fell for her lips. The Hollywood red she wore, like the screen stars of the fifties, gave her an irresistible carmine velvet smile.

I proposed immediately, just after our third encounter. I felt good and calm in her presence; it felt smooth and enchanting when her red lips touched my face. Her kisses had the taste of some rare old wine and I believed then that her lips and her make-up bag would erase the memory of death and its smell for ever. I thought my enchantment would last eternally. I only regretted that her name was Margot and not Ruby.

'My Ruby' were the words I used when I had a sudden surge of affection for my wife and when I needed to convey my deep love to her. But these words sounded like betrayal and carried a nostalgic silence that weighed discreetly on our love and on our life together. These two words came out of my mouth and infiltrated every bit of me like a permanent depression. I have never betrayed my wife, but I incessantly felt like a cheat, and the sense of deceit became more painfully acute each time I felt passionately attached to her. For I really care for my wife, and I owe her every bit of soothing and securing happiness I have enjoyed in my life since I was sent, as a young soldier, to Belsen.

But death and cruelty don't just visit you. They are like nasty bites; you forget about them for a short while, before they haunt you in your skin, making your life miserable again. The red interludes have kept me going, though, and I do love my wife, I love her lips. We are old now, I have even lost the taste for water and her lips are thinner; they have lost their shiny temptress look, but they are still smiling under their matte coat of orange-red and I am still appeased when I look at them.

I look at her lips and I remember that flowers are still growing in our garden and that we are still around; she with her lipsticks getting paler and more discreet with the years passing and me squeezing my eyes a bit tighter every day, a bit harder so that the colour of Ruby's red lips, that has kept me going, does not fade away before I die.

Red as in taboo, the colour of safety codes and their transgressions. Red, the pleasure of high risk, emergency and prohibition. Long-lasting red, as in survival. Red, loud red screams 'I exist.'

In Time of War

We live in a time when war, far from being eliminated from the planet, is a continuing fact of life for many. Some wars are overt military operations, others are endemic situations of social and economic conflict.

What can artists do when there is a war?

Ezra Pound's answer: 'Ask me what a rose bush is for.'

Jeannette Winterson asked on the eve of this war: 'Do rose bushes matter in a war? What can art do for us now?'

I know there is a sneaking feeling, even among art lovers, that art is a luxury. While pictures, books, music and theatre are not quite handmade luggage or perfume, most people wouldn't admit that art is essential. The endless rows over funding centre on an insecurity about the role of art in society. Nobody doubts that hospitals and schools must be paid for by all of us. Mention art, and the answer seems to be that it should rely on the marketplace; let those who want it pay for it. Art is specialised, particular, elitist and probably bogus. In Britain, a few old masters – Shakespeare and Dickens, Mozart and Puccini – are enough to feed the general interest in the arts.

Like God, it fails us continually. Like God, we have legitimate doubts about its existence but, like God, art leaves us with footprints of beauty. We sense there is more to life than the material world can provide, and art is a clue, an intimation at its best, a transformation. We don't need to believe in it, but we can experience it. The experience suggests that the monolith of corporate culture is only a partial reality. This is important information, and art provides it.

When you take time to read a book or listen to music or look at a picture, the first thing you are doing is turning your attention inwards. The outside world, with all of its demands, has to wait. Art begins to reach you with energies of its own ... This is not simply about being recharged, as in a good night's sleep or a holiday; it is about being charged at a completely different voltage ... Art's counterculture, however diverse, holds in plain sight what the material world denies – love and imagination. Art can bring us back to consciousness, sometimes quietly, sometimes dramatically, but the responsibility to act on what we find is ours.

Why did the Taliban bullet down the Buddhas? Why did Hitler burn books? Why was *Ulysses* banned? Why did Franco refuse to show *Guernica*? Art is potent, confrontational, difficult ...

Don't be fooled by the way capitalism co-opts art. It pretends to do it for money, but underneath money is terror – terror that there might be a different way to live. There is a different way, and it's not a William Morris utopia, or an Omega workshop niche; it's a celebration of the human spirit. Art reminds us of all the possibilities we are persuaded to forget. Peace or war, we need those alternatives.

Howard Zinn has this to say about art and war, this war:

I hadn't been in a war yet but it [Art] brought war home to me in a very vivid way. This is what art does, this is what Goya's paintings did, what writers who write about war, Erich Maria Remarque's *All*

Quiet on the Western Front, movies, the poetry of e.e. cummings and Wilfred Owen. Art is a substitute for personal experience. It can bring people close to an experience even though they've never had the experience and almost make them feel how it really was. We've got to use art in every possible way to bring home to people what the war would be like. What happened in the Vietnam War, people who had never seen war saw the photos of the victims of the My Lai massacre. They saw the photos of the kid walking down the street with the napalmed skin falling off her. The war was brought home to them through art, through photographs, through literature. So that's what will have to be done in this situation to make the American people realize that this is not just 'oh, we're going to war, period' as an abstraction. Bush sees it as an abstraction. Not only has Bush never been in a war, but I don't think he's ever experienced an artistic rendering of war in a way that would move him in any way.

London

I visited London for the first time some twenty-five years ago. Like many Lebanese then, I had fled Lebanon, where a terrible civil war had made it impossible for people like me, who didn't belong to any clan, to fit in or survive. I came to London from Paris to discover a very cosmopolitan city where many nationalities and ethnic groups coexisted, among them many Arabs, from the Middle East to North Africa. Rich Arabs, poor Arabs, students, intellectuals, professionals: in other words, a multitude of small Arab societies were settling or had already settled in London. There were many food shops, all the ingredients we needed to cook our home cuisine, there were newspapers, tapes of classical and popular songs, there was even a cinema showing Arab films every day ... One thing I couldn't see, one major aspect of Arab cultural life, was books.

To be fair to the British book world, one could find books on Arabic literature, or in Arabic, but these books were for an elite that read the classics. One could easily find many editions of *A Thousand and One Nights*, *Kalila and Dimna*, *The Seances of al-Hariri*, the works of a few classical poets, and even – thanks to Burton, and less to Mrs Burton, who'd helped to censor the spiciest bits – more than one edition of *The Perfumed Gardens*, the erotic essay by Sheikh Nefzaoui.

Arab cultural life was very poorly and archaically represented to say the least in those days. The books one could read said nothing about the Arab world as I knew it. To recognise it I would have had to be at least 900 years old.

But today, here in London, in this library, I feel totally different. I feel totally at home, if I may say. And I am happy. Not only because among all these books and all these worlds they tell us about, I can distract myself from the terrible carnage that happened a few days ago in New York. Not only because I can forget for a while the dangers of a future where the word 'war' is increasingly common and ever more threatening. But because standing among these books I feel I am living in many epochs, witnessing a multitude of realities, and because the collection of Arabic books exhibited or available, and that are translated into English, speak more sincerely about the reality of the Middle East.

Here, I have to be subjective and speak of my bias towards literature and novels. I love literature, not only because it is entertaining, but also because it speaks the language of individuals to individuals. When I'm reading a book translated from Spanish, Japanese or Urdu, late at night in bed, I'm on my own, away from my environmental influences; I'm left with the characters of my novel, I'm interacting with them for the whole length of the book. I cannot, even if I wanted to, generalise, look at them with my society's prejudices, or turn them into clichés. Novels humanise their readers.

Here in this library you can discover a more realistic Arab world than the one we see or hear through the news. In the books of Naguib Mahfouz we can live the life of a typical middle-class Cairene family. We can feel the dramatic tension between a mother and her son, her only protector, and the difficulties for him in loving sexually a woman he respects like his mother. With Ghada al-Samman or Nawal al-Sadaawi, we can hear the revolted scream of an Arab woman claiming her right to her sexual freedom. We can live Arab history through adventures and romances with Amin Maalouf. We can go through an Algerian childhood with Assia Djabbar. Here, through literature, we can know the Arab world in its reality, through the imagination and dreams of its storytellers.

I do agree with Kundera that the novel is a European invention. But I would add that this fantastic European invention has pervaded the world; it had become global before the word 'globalisation' became fashionable. Moreover, the Arab novel has benefited from the influence of the West as well as from its local tradition of storytelling, or the infinite love of the word in Arabic culture and poetry.

You need only read Taher Ben Jalloun to see how one can write Arabic in a European language and offer the world a literary masterpiece.

Finally, I look around and I feel that my efforts and the efforts of my colleagues at Saqi Books have not been in vain. When we started Saqi we believed that books were the best tools to create a rapprochement between people. We wanted to be a *carrefour*, a roundabout, where languages met, where one could no longer tell where the East starts and where the West ends. By translating French, English, Spanish books into Arabic and by publishing Middle Eastern and African writers in English, we have found a place on this roundabout. Our books have found a home in nice places like this library, and this gives me a lot of hope in a time when the word 'divergent' is more popular than 'diversity'.

Lebanon: Slices of Life

Driving with Rida

Rida is a character that only Martin Scorsese or John Updike could have created. But Rida is not a fictional creation; he is a Lebanese driver and he is very real. As he takes me through the messy roads of Beirut, Rida complains. He scorns the other drivers and those who allow them to carry a driving licence, he protests about the cost of living, he curses the government. His diatribes always end with the same conclusion: 'Our politicians are thieves and if we were in a civilised country, they'd all have been hanged by now'.

Rida is from the south of Lebanon and lives in the *dahiya* (southern suburbs) of Beirut. For me, he is a great source to catch the mood in Lebanon, and despite the repetitions, whenever I sit in his car, I do my best to trigger a conversation by asking, 'What do you think will happen to us in this country?'

I know that before elaborating he will confirm to me that nothing good is to be expected. This time I ask Rida where he escaped with his family during the Israeli invasion and what he thinks about the resistance movement. Tales of heroism start to pour from the driver's mouth.

'We taught Israel a lesson; every person was ready to sacrifice their life, *fida Sayyid Nasrallah*.' (*Fida* means 'giving one's life for'.)

'But Rida,' I ask, 'what happened to your home?'

As the traffic thickens and the hold-ups increase (another by-product of the disappearance of bridges in the country), Rida's frustration rises to a crescendo.

'I don't know what all this was for. When you have a criminal neighbour like Israel, you should think a hundred times before provoking it. Hizbollah should have known better – what heroism is there in creating a million refugees? Believe me, *sitna* (dear lady), if they had not distributed compensation money to the people who had their homes destroyed, they would have been spat upon by all the Shi'i population.'

I didn't suggest to Rida that this was an exaggeration, for Rida always exaggerates. I didn't tell him that within five minutes he had confidently expressed two directly opposing positions. I didn't tell him that because, after a few days in Lebanon, I had realised that many people proclaim completely contradictory views within a short conversation. People's identifications and convictions are dual, if not multiple, and after the war they all speak and behave as if they had survived an earthquake or some traumatic natural disaster.

Rida's wife has decided to wear a veil, he says with a slightly proud smile, even though he has never asked her to do so. He also tells me a joke that is circulating in Lebanon: he displays the V sign using his index and his middle finger and asks, 'What does this mean?', immediately answering, 'There are only two buildings left.'

After successive destructive wars, the Lebanese are masters in black humour.

The second day I asked Rida to drive me to the mountains in the Metn, a Maronite (Christian) area north of Beirut. It was Saturday, 14 October, and General Michel Aoun, the Christian ally of Hizbollah, had called for a big rally the next day. His aim was to display his ability to mobilise the masses, both Christian and Shi'i, and ultimately to become the president of the republic (in the event, heavy rainfall forced the rally's abandonment).

Again, jokes are running fast among Lebanese Christians, which reflect the political atmosphere better than any analysis. One goes like this: General Aoun calls his aide and asks him to prepare two hundred sandwiches for the people at the rally. His aide says, 'But general, we are expecting two hundred thousand demonstrators – why only two hundred sandwiches?' 'Because all the others are fasting for Ramadan,' says the general (meaning that the masses Aoun can mobilise are actually the masses Hizbollah will mobilise for him).

When we reach Antelias, we see in this Christian enclave next to General Aoun a sea of orange flags and a huge Hizbollah banner hanging in the middle of the place. I look at Rida's face and see it beaming with pleasure. When I ask him why he is so pleased, he replies, 'It is nice to see us featured in this area.'

'Us?' I ask. You have been complaining about Hizbollah and its adventurous attack and its responsibility for all the misery of the Shi'i population all through the trip from Beirut to Antelias! I don't understand.'

'Well,' he says, 'who would have dreamed of seeing a Shi'i party celebrated in this area!'

That is why it is great to speak to Rida. He is representative of all the contradictory identities of the Lebanese, their variegated belonging to their nation, community and individuality. Rida complains about all his affiliations, but 'affiliated' he nonetheless is.

On the terrace

It is still hot in Beirut in early October. When I visit Nada and Samir, I ask to have our drink on the balcony. They live in west Beirut, in a traditionally Sunni area that is now Shi'i as well. It is Ramadan, but the supermarket down the road still sells me a bottle of wine that we intend to enjoy on their terrace.

Other friends join us. The *Husseiniya* (Shi'i mosque) next door has a powerful loudspeaker and the sheikh starts his prayers. My host complains, 'Each evening during Ramadan we have to endure listening to this monotonous chanting for two or three hours! This shouldn't be permitted.'

His wife says that at least they could have selected a sheikh with a better voice.

The other guests start to tell stories about how it is becoming impossible to complain about the zealots who are overextending the prayers and overusing the capacity of the loudspeakers. Samir goes inside and puts some *tarab* (Arabic blues) in his CD player. We end up discussing politics, the 'terrible situation' and exchanging the latest jokes in the midst of a musical cacophony.

My friends are secular and all complain about the ascending power of the religious groups in the country. Mohammad, a university teacher, disagrees with them all.

'I was against Hizbollah and its attack, but once Israel attacked I supported the resistance. Now I am happy the international forces are here, for what would happen to us secular Muslims if we were left with a triumphant and omnipresent Hizbollah?'

I listen quietly for once and remind them that they can still drink their whiskey quite comfortably in the middle of Ramadan and that this is possible because Lebanon is still holding it together as a country.

Another terrace, in east Beirut this time. A beautiful view of the city can be seen from the terrace of Zeina, a fashion designer. She receives her customers in her home, and always invites them to enjoy the sight from her terrace before displaying her latest designs. Her customers are always seduced by the panoramic view of Beirut; but today Zeina isn't smiling back with pride when we compliment her on her location.

'I can't sleep any longer,' she says, 'A new nightclub opened a few weeks ago, and even if I close all the windows, the pop music and the synthesisers assault my eardrums till four a.m. every morning. I've been complaining every day to the owner and to the gendarmerie, but to no avail. They are not going to kick me out of my flat.'

We all sympathised, but know quite well that she has no chance of winning her battle. The nightclub owners are very generous towards the police and the heads of local gendarmeries. Even though she runs a successful business, and even if she was willing to bribe a policeman, she'd never be able to compete with the most successful businesses in Lebanon: restaurants and nightclubs.

I look at her designs and remember my evening at Nada and Samir's. From west to east Beirut, people are complaining about noise on their balcony. Does it matter if the source is religious or secular? Does it matter if its source is the throat of a sheikh or the strings of an electric guitar? In Lebanon, sadly, it sometimes does!

Cultural scenes

An art gallery that was not deterred by the dangers of war. Two young women defy the depressive mood of the Lebanese intelligentsia and curators and organise an exhibition of art created during the war. It is small, simple, but very touching.

Installations, collages, sculptures and video art speak of the war between Hizbollah and Israel, or more accurately of the artists' concerns during the war. I spent more than an hour browsing through the gallery, always returning and stopping, intrigued, in front of an installation called 'A House That Anne Frank Did Not Live In, And Books She Did Not Write.'

The artist is from the south and he has piled all the remains of his torn and burned books on the floor of the gallery; an Israeli bomb had fallen on his home, turning it into rubble. Why this title? Is he saying that the Israelis are doing to us what the Nazis did to the Jews? Is he complaining that we are suffering like Anne Frank, but that our suffering is not recognised? The books he had in his home speak of the latest artistic tendencies exhibited in museums all over the world. The artist is obviously connected, so is Lebanon after all. Will it still be true?

This time I felt a sort of tiredness among the Lebanese, a deep sense of desperation.

'Don't tell us that we Lebanese always get back on our feet. We don't want to have to always rebuild, we're fed up of having initiative,' said Najwa to a journalist who was trying to be supportive.

Many art works are ironic. Black humour again. On the way out of the gallery I feel better, somehow stronger. But art always does this to me.

Al-Wilaya is Hizbollah's official group of singers and musicians. They are performing everywhere and, were it not for piracy (according to the studio owner in the southern suburb), they would have sold millions of recordings of their latest CD, rather than just half a million.

Listen to their lead singer speaking: 'We use drums, synthesisers, trumpets, clarinets, but not tambourines or *derboukas* [drums]. These encourage dance. They [meaning "the West", I guess] think we are ignorant and backward but we are cultured. We love life, music and art. We don't just live for martyrdom and death. But we want to live with dignity and pride.'

The problem is that synthesisers are not exactly authentic Arab or Islamic musical instruments, while the *derbouka* is. But in any case, I believe that Islamic movements nowadays are an expression of postmodernity and not at all a recurrence of things past. The word 'fundamentalist' is misleading.

When I am ready to face it, Hassan takes me to the southern suburbs. They are lively again. Many young people are walking back from school, avoiding the piles of rubble and the holes left by the Israeli bombs. Not all the women are veiled. Many are wearing tight jeans and showing off their stylish coiffures. Anger and sadness compete inside me to the point of nausea. How could anybody do this to a heavily populated area?

I had seen the pictures on TV, but none of them had shown the dresses or the blouses or the toys still caught in the piles of concrete that were people's homes. Hassan had his home bombed but is still living in it, avoiding the hole in the middle of his son's bedroom.

'Why are you living in your home still?' I ask him. 'You can rent a flat away from the *dahiya* until you renovate your flat.'

'I want to be home, I am used to it here, this is my neighbourhood.'

Hassan came to the *dahiya* after being evicted from the flat he had occupied downtown (which he had moved into when he lost his home during an earlier war). I remembered the Palestinians, who felt nostalgic for their camps when they were obliged to leave Lebanon. Home is where you have built habits; old traditions are often quite recent.

One building is cut in half, revealing a display of white wedding dresses. The shop is trying to do business, as if to prove that life is made of celebrations and funerals. A hairdressing salon has an advertising sign made of a Fernando Botero painting next to a shop selling clothes for the *muhajjabat* (veiled women). At every corner there is a large poster celebrating the 'divine victory'. I had a feeling I was walking through a Salvador Dali painting, a sad, bizarre painting.

To the south, but food first ...

Before heading south I visit Souk al-Tayeb. It is Saturday and Kamal is still refusing to be defeated by the war. Kamal is a sweet, elegant and generous person who loves food and takes pleasure in all things culinary. When I meet him in Souk al-Tayeb, the organic heaven he has created, he kisses me and says: 'Don't leave this country. Look at all these displays of wonderful food that people have brought here.'

I look around and see an enormous variety of homemade products being cooked or sold in this picturesque souk in the middle of the

Solidere area. Kamal is also trying to celebrate Lebanese apples because the agricultural sector has suffered huge losses (from chemical damage to crops, and from the cluster-bombs that have killed more than twenty children since the war ended and left farmers too afraid to pick their crops).

The Lebanese are obsessive about good cuisine. They discuss and taste dishes endlessly. Within half an hour in the souk I tasted two delicious sweets that I had never previously encountered or even heard of. I learn that Kamal had also organised Souk al-Tuffah (a souk of apples) and a competition for new recipes using apples. The winner had invented a wonderful dish of vine leaves stuffed with apples.

One thing is sure, the glorious food tradition of the Lebanese has not been beaten by this bloody war. It is still feverishly alive.

Nabil and Samia pick me up for the journey to the south of Lebanon. The road will be long, much longer than usual, as there are no bridges left, thanks to the Israelis' hateful attack. I am furious at the sight and scale of the destruction. Nabil cheers me up with another input of black humour. During the war, he hired a taxi to take him to Sidon to bring his mother to Beirut. Approaching a bridge, the taxi driver (who already had charged Nabil ten times the normal price) asks, 'Sir, would you rather die under the bridge or over it?'

Cooking

I've always dreamt of being a good cook. Actually, for a long time now my wish has been to be a *great* cook, an incredibly fantastic cook. My friends, especially those who've put all their energies and talents into their professional or artistic careers, don't take my culinary ambitions too seriously.

'Why do you care so much about being a good cook?' 'You've hardly enough time to move from your desk to your studio.' 'You don't need to bother with new chores,' they keep telling me.

Well, let me tell you what I don't dare tell my friends: they are absolutely wrong and, to say the least, naïve! To put it in milder terms, they have no clue about art and the essence of what makes a real artist.

An artist produces beauty, and a tasty dish is beauty itself. Art is generous, and what could ever be more generous than a work of art that is to be consumed in joy and not destined to last eternally and for posterity?

Please don't raise your eyebrows or revert to polemics of the kind

I heard two days ago: 'What happened to women's lib' and the cause of women?' 'We've fought for years to be freed from our kitchens and now you want us to go creative on the stove and perform next to the fridge?'

These are the arguments of those who either understood nothing about the women's movement or who never questioned why all great chefs are men. Unfortunately, until now, women feed their families when they fry and boil and serve, while men exercise the art of cooking when they do the same. Women are at home when they cook, while men are employed in restaurants. So let's not hide behind feminist terminology when we speak of starters, main dishes and desserts.

'You want to be like Zarifa, when you can be a Louise?' asked my friend Lyn. Sitt Zarifa is the woman who cooked for her grandmother and her mother's family in Beirut, and is now cooking for Lyn's own family in London. And Louise, as you may have guessed, is Louise Bourgeois, the great sculptor who is the star and the dear of the art world today, getting more creative now that she's in her eighties.

I don't know Louise Bourgeois. I know her installations and her huge sculptures, and I've read about her quite a lot. But I know Zarifa in flesh and blood. Zarifa has given me and all of Lyn's friends great moments of happiness and pleasure, both for the eyes and the palate. Sitt Zarifa! I can see her smile while she carries her famous tagine to our table. A real work of art, Zarifa's tagine. An oasis of white, sparkling with golden stars. Those who have no imagination and no romanticism might describe it as a dish of tahina with fried pine kernels, but the art connoisseurs will see a glittering display of colour contrasts and an ingenious harmony of soft and crunchy textures. And look at Zarifa's face when Lyn's guests mutter '*mmm*' and 'great' while savouring and chatting and sating their hunger! It's the most generous smile I've ever seen on a person's face. I find it hard to believe that Louise would have such a glow in her eyes when exhibiting her giant spider sculpture or her new installation. But who knows. Praising

Zarifa shouldn't make me speculate on the other artist, who instead of working with olive oil and cumin works with plaster or iron.

I did say they were both artists, and I do believe it. But I have to admit that there is a difference. While Zarifa's long hours of labour are consumed by our eyes and our palates, Louise's work will survive for ever. So will Louise's name. The same cannot be said about Sitt Zarifa. Soon nobody will remember her name, not even if her recipes find their way into our future civilisations. Zarifa is more like a performance artist, her artistic output lasting only for a short while, the duration of a meal. And the satisfied smile of Zarifa while she sees her work being consumed at great speed speaks of an immense generosity, often lost within the egos of other types of artists.

Yesterday I understood Zarifa and all the great women who spend hours decorating cakes that will pass into oblivion within minutes. I had a few friends come for dinner and I decided to give them the best I could do for my table. The food was good, the table looked pretty, people ate, laughed, *hummed* and *mmmed* and had second helpings. It felt warm and pleasurable and intimate and spicy, and life felt worth living and everybody seemed great and nice. How many books or paintings can achieve such a miracle? A few, no doubt, but not that often.

If Lyn asks me the question again, I won't hesitate before answering who I'd rather be, Zarifa or Louise.

Missed Opportunities: Me and My Gender

It took me a long time to understand why my mother loved to tell the story of the doctor who delivered me. Whenever there was a willing audience, she would tell it. I must have heard it a thousand times.

For her story to make sense, you need to know that I am the second female born to my parents and that my sister and I are their only progeny.

'When Dr Razook left the delivery room, his face was tense and he walked past your father without looking at him. Your father was waiting anxiously for the baby to be delivered so that he could join me. [In those days, husbands were never allowed to witness the birth of their child]. The look on the doctor's face terrified your father, who thought that something terrible must have happened to me and to our baby. When he knew that I had delivered a healthy baby girl, he was delighted. Dr Razook didn't like to deliver girls, especially if the parents were his friends, and he felt his reputation as a gynaecologist was perturbed by every female he brought into this world. For your dad and me, we didn't care one way or the other, boy or girl.'

The story of my birth as told by my mother is a perfect metaphor for my country of origin. It is the story of juxtaposed values and contradictions. Yes, it is OK to be born a girl, but the story doesn't end there. There is a 'but', a Mediterranean 'but', and a westernised 'OK' that have to coexist and modernised citizens somehow have to juggle and survive within the spaces of this coexistence. And they have do it with grace and honour. My parents are from the generation of Middle Easterners who lived at a time of transition from the traditional values of large families to the westernised nuclear family with a maximum of two children, raised and educated in the best schools you could afford. They dreamt of bringing up free, responsible individuals – individuals who were nonetheless constantly reminded that they were the custodians of their family's honour, especially if they stood on the female side of the gender border; individuals who had to watch constantly for 'what the neighbours say' about them and their parents, their uncles, cousins and other relatives.

My story, the way I tried to live my life, is a desperate, not always unhappy, effort to reconcile at least two epochs, two modes of behaviour, two value systems that prevailed simultaneously and very concretely in pre-war Lebanon.

Let me come back to my mother. A clever woman, who was considered very marriageable thanks to her good looks, and who was consequently withdrawn from school, in the late 1940s, by her parents at the age of sixteen. She had loved her school and treasured the knowledge she had acquired there, mainly in the sciences. She had no say about her parents' decision, and anyway, she had fallen in love with my father. My father, a modern young man, cared very little about the difference in their religious confessions and courted her openly because he had 'good intentions'. They fell madly in love and married when she was seventeen and he twenty years old. They despised marriages of convenience or calculation, believed in true love and had the Hollywood movies, already triumphant over the screens of Beirut, to confirm the righteousness of their romantic choice.

There were a few couples like them in Lebanon in those days, but they were not the rule. Nine months after their wedding, they brought my older sister into this world. They were delighted; they adored her. One only has to look at the infinite number of pictures they took of her, and at the journal my mother kept, in which she recorded every smile, every tooth that appeared on the baby girl's face. It occurred to me once that the same Dr Razook had delivered my sister, and that he may have been as disappointed by this deed as he was when it was my turn to show up. But, for some unexplained reason, it was only my appearance that seemed to be a worthy story for my mother to narrate. The reason should have been obvious to me. It may not matter to the parents if the newborn is male or female, but in the wider society there is nothing to boast about when you bring only girls into the Middle Eastern world. You have to be very keen on bringing up a small, well-cared-for family to stop after the second child and not try for that special one that will perpetuate your name and speak for the virility of the father and the blessing of the mother.

Garçon manqué was the term I kept hearing about me. Tomboy. The French expression is more revealing. A boy missed. An opportunity missed. But the values that the post-industrial societies had introduced in our Levantine reality were tangible enough, and no third child was to be expected. So my story meets that of my society. I am female, accepted as such but unconsciously or very silently wished different. The context in which I was born, the Lebanon of the 1950s, was a paradigm of this dichotomy. Some named the two poles in this combination modern and traditional, others used the labels east and west; now the term post-modern is frequently used.

I can think of a perfect metaphor: *un garçon manqué*, a missed boy and *une opportunité manquée*, a missed opportunity. A country that has missed its democratic and tolerant potentialities. A happy alternative. But ...

To go back to my gender and its implications: like any child who finds him/herself at the centre of attention, I started to play the role that made me successful among the members of my family and their friends. I started to behave as a tomboy. I wrote to Father Christmas asking him for a cowboy outfit. When I played with my dolls I did so discreetly, for the pleasure of mothering or dressing them was hampered by a sharp feeling of guilt and the fear of disappointing the grown-ups. I joined the boys in the courtyard after school to play football and all was free and fun until Sitt Zalfa, an imposing old neighbour, saw me fighting physically over the score with one of the boys. She used to terrify us with her severe chignon and her Turkish and Italian vocabulary. '*Pronto*!' she screamed, pointing her stick at me and then in the direction of my home. She visited my parents and told them that it was not 'right' for a nine-year-old girl to mix with the boys of the neighbourhood. That was the end of my street life. What the neighbours said proved more powerful than the cute image of a *garçon manqué*. The neighbours' opinion had a decisive influence on my parents, who still insisted that it did not matter to them if I were a girl or a boy. We were already in the early 1960s, and Lebanon enjoyed the rule of a functioning parliament; a *coup d'état* had been defeated and my mother, as well as my aunts, dressed in the latest Parisian fashions. My mixed school was preparing to separate the girls from the boys: yes, even the French *lyceé* adapted its rules to the Arab-Mediterranean reality of Lebanese society. Religion and religious teaching were not allowed inside the secular institution, but girls who were approaching puberty had to be separated from boys. A *garçon manqué* in a girls' school did not make much sense. A segregated secular *lyceé* would have been an anomaly in France, but we were not in France, even though we spoke French and believed in the values of the Enlightenment.

I had heard my parents calling me a tomboy, and now I started hearing my mother asserting that I was very good in the sciences, the objective ones. Accordingly I became good at mathematics and physics. My grades in French literature, a subject I adored, did not impress my mother, whereas her face would beam with joy whenever she saw me resolving some geometry or calculus problem. This was a safer way of replacing the boy that was never to be born; safer than playing and fighting with the boys over a football kick. For sciences do not jeopardise virtue or reputation. At school, when I was not yet fourteen years old, I read *The Mandarins* of Simone de Beauvoir and heard of free love, but the concert by Johnny Halliday, the French pop star, had been cancelled by the Minister of the Interior, the 'progressive' Kamal Jumblatt who believed that 'western degenerate images' did not suit our moral values and might be harmful to our youth. Along with all the citizens of Lebanon in the 1960s, I learned to live with these conflicting attitudes and values. Jugglers we became: with more or less graciousness, sometimes over some broken eggs, we wove our way through miniskirts and scarves, chanting anti-imperialist slogans as well as the Beatles. The kitsch singer Taroub sang for an Arab public, while her sister Mayada set Arabic words to western pop music. When a dance called the *Hully Gully* invaded the nightclubs of Lebanon, the famous Diva Sabah sang *Hully Dabke Yaba Of*:

Hully Gully est connu chez tous les occidentaux,
Hully Dabke Yaba Of est connu chez
Les Orientaux, presque le meme et tout le monde l'aime.

Neither we nor Sabah could have guessed that the Occident and the Orient were going to sing to totally different tunes. From Radio Cairo the mesmerising voice of Umm Kulthum was asking for a rifle – *A'tini Bunduqiya* – a rifle to liberate Arab land. We were reading Jean-Paul Sartre and starting to demonstrate for the liberation of Palestine.

By the early 1970s I was studying mathematics and French literature. Male and female subjects. Feminism was on the agenda: George Tarabishi translated Sheila Rowbotham, Germaine Greer's *The Female Eunuch* was available in the bookshops and Sonia Beiruti, a TV broadcaster, invited a few of us onto her TV show to debate women's emancipation. Two scenes from that period keep recurring in my memory. First scene: on this TV show I said I wanted to be a free woman and to be independent, to work so that I would not live off my father's or a future husband's money. My father, who was watching the programme, felt deeply humiliated. He understood these words as an insult to his honour. Second scene: during a student demonstration a few women jumped onto the shoulders of their colleagues to lead and chant revolutionary slogans. Everybody in this demonstration had seen the pictures of May 1968 in France and the dynamic images of the women lifted above the crowds by their co-objectors. 'Scandalous,' screamed some passers-by, as well as a few demonstrators. The women were put down very quickly. We may have been influenced by May 1968 but we were not in the Latin Quarter of Paris; we were still on the shores of the Mediterranean.

We were a parliamentary democracy, we had no kings and no army generals ruling over us, but many of our politicians were the sons of landowners, or sons of other politicians. They all spoke of democracy, and we called for our right to independence as women while armed militias were being formed and operations to restore women's virginity were easily available. Somehow, I see a parallel between my studying mathematics at the American University and French literature at the Lebanese National University, between my gender that held me responsible for the family's reputation on the one hand and my country's coexisting contradictions on the other.

Feminism was an obvious route to follow for somebody like me – a woman who had believed that men's spaces were not totally impermeable, nor mysterious or difficult to handle. You play with boys, enter their classrooms, obtain better grades than many of them and then you are asked to obey them or accept an inequality that places them above you? This was very difficult to swallow, especially if Simone de Beauvoir's *The Second Sex* has been widely read among your French-educated friends and her assertion that *'on ne naît pas une femme, on le devient'* (one is not born a woman, one becomes so) is a cool slogan to raise. Old feminism, that of the pioneers such as Hoda Sha'rawi or the active lawyer Laure Meghayzel, felt inadequate to our youthful impatience. We did not want only equality, the right to be professional while ensuring that we were first and foremost 'good mothers': we wanted to claim loudly and shamelessly that nothing could stop us from realising our wishes and that our bodies belonged to us.

Engels, Reich and Alexandra Kollontai's teachings gave a social dimension to our belief that 'all is possible'. The country itself believed that its growth as the financial-tourist heaven for the Middle East and its enriched Gulf region was unstoppable, that the Palestinian resistance fighters were the local expression of the Vietnamese freedom fighters. We spoke loudly against the hypocrisy of our society. We were getting more radicalised in our beliefs, and so were the contradictions and the conflicts in Lebanon.

A time came when, in the middle of the bloody and cruel sequences of the civil war, I started to miss the so-called hypocrisy of pre-war times. The feeling that 'I want everything and I want it now' dissipated. I looked with different eyes on the liberalism of my parents who had to bite on their Mediterranean wound and let me be. They tolerated my freedom of movement, even though my tomboy image was long dead and buried under the powerful influence of Sitt Zalfa and her ilk.

I moved to the other side of the Green Line where I thought people would be free from the prejudices of my own milieu. There I found a reversed mirror detonating with the same kind of intolerance. What we called hypocrisy before the war was the best form of compromise people had found for living together. The taboo preventing one spelling out one's dislike for the other had been a good discipline. Look around you and see how ugly it all becomes when people feel no inhibition in their intolerance. I am not calling for censorship, far from that. People have the right to express their feelings, however despicable we may think them, but this should not discourage us from doing all we can to relate hatred for the other's colour, race or sexual choice to the notion of bad, uncivilised and immoral, and to link the violent expression of this hatred to legal judgment and action.

Yes, it took me a long time to realise why my mother loved to tell the story of Dr Razook and my birth. It took me longer to realise that the contradictions my parents had to live through opened great new spaces for me. And if they had not hoped for me to jump over the limiting fences my gender imposed on me, I may have been confined to living, all my life, on one side of the border(s) and I would have never learned that we were all as human or as bad as 'the other' during the ugly years of our civil war. If my mother had not told this story, would I have had the confidence, some eighteen years ago, to face the London bank manager who was reluctant to deal with me as one of the directors of Saqi Books and 'would rather see my male boss'? Would I have had the courage to bend the long aluminium rod that holds my sculptures, would I have been capable of being 'the other', of integrating with 'the others' without pain and often with plenty of fun? I may have been a missed opportunity for Dr Razook and others like him, but I still believe that I am better off missing the narrowness of the choice that would have been my secure lot and instead taking the risk of following my individual routes.

Beauty, Pain and Martyrdom

I am the martyr Sanaa Yousef Mehaidli. I am seventeen years old.
I am not dead ... I am alive, I am with you. I sing ... I dance ... I am
fulfilling all my wishes ... I am so happy to be a heroic martyr ...
I beg you not to cry, not to be sad. On the contrary, be happy, keep
on smiling to a world as long as this world has heroes. I am now
planted in the soil of the south, irrigating it with my blood and my
love.

This is how Sanaa spoke to us posthumously through the TV screen
on 15 March 1985. She had recorded her speech on video before
blowing herself up in a suicidal operation against the Israeli army in
the south of Lebanon.

Oh Mother, how happy I shall be when my bones will be scattered
through my flesh, when my blood will flow in the earth of the
south ... Do not feel angry with me leaving our home without
informing you, my parents ... I have not left to get married, or

to live with somebody; I left home to become an honourable, courageous, happy martyr.

My testament is my name: The Bride of the South.

Sanaa Mehaidli was one of the first women to go on a suicide mission in the Middle East. She was a member of a nationalist party, a secular party. I still hear the words: blood, pure, bride, martyr. They haunt me.

Her posthumous words on the screen spoke of the body in pain, the body annihilated, and the more Sanaa seemed happy for us to see her suicidal body celebrated, the more my anguish about the integrity of the body, my own body included, increased.

The Bride of the South sounded ecstatic. She wanted us to celebrate her death as if we were celebrating her wedding. The Virgin of the South, as a few enthusiastic broadcasters kept calling her, was telling us that there is beauty and enjoyment in martyrdom. The blood, the red fluid that she spread, was that of her 'purity'.

Red for Sanaa and those who walked shouting slogans at her funeral/wedding; red, the colour of bleeding veins, is also the colour of action and revelry. Red, bright, diurnal, is a spur to action, says the *Dictionary of Symbols*; it is also the basis of the taboos relating to menstruating women. Red is not the colour of weddings in the Middle East, but Sanaa and her comrades adopted it as the colour of festivities, of morbid enjoyment. Sanaa's death is that of all martyrs, it is a wishful attempt at eternity on this earth; it is like the wishes of art or of the kind of art that expects to be written with a capital 'A'.

'They are not dead,' screamed the poet walking behind the martyrs' coffin:

They are not dead
They are all alive
The earth and the skies chant their names
The night covers their faces and takes them away

But their souls prevail
For they are light.[1]

Some men are born posthumously, says Nietzsche, but some, like Sanaa, try to live through death. For those who did not see the torn bodies, did not smell the burnt flesh, the decaying blood, Sanaa's loss of blood is described as love-making. The blood she spilled is that of her virginity.

If beauty is a tormented and debatable notion where the visualised body is at stake, the smell never lies.

I cannot engage in the subject of beauty and pain without writing with my body, with my guts more than with my intellect. The awesome or tragic register of the beautiful in wars, in martyrs' torments and the sacrificial is a register of fear and attraction; it is a state that brings together anger and fascination, a reproduction of an obscure dream, an obscure object of (abject) desire. Susan Sontag knows this feeling and she expresses it in the most clairvoyant and succinct terms:

To find beauty in war photographs seems heartless. But the landscape of devastation is still a landscape ... and as an image something may be beautiful – or terrifying, or unbearable, or quite bearable – as it is not in real life.

I feel the urge to add one phrase to Sontag's lines. I need to say this: It is because in real life the landscape of devastation is also the smell of this devastation.

The smell of morbidity has never been celebrated. Indeed, martyrdom has been depicted by painters, religious and non-religious sculptors, romantic and enflamed colourists in images that are odourless. The pictures and the posters of martyrs are often framed with flowery designs, blue skies and white flying feathers. They speak already of paradise, and paradise smells of musk, not of burning flesh.

---

1.   N. Fayad, for the martyrs of independence from the Ottomans in Lebanon

The blood of the martyr smells of dusk ...

Bury the Martyr in his clothes. The clothes he was wearing when he died. For he should not be separated from his wounds and his blood. He should meet his God bearing the marks of his heroic sacrifices. The world exhibits plenty of attractions, it has many wonders that can attract the eye and steal the heart. Money and gold and pretty women, they all play with man's soul and reason. But when the knowledge of God is well rooted in a man's heart, all these attractions turn into despicable ghosts. The pleasure of knowing God is the most delectable pleasure ever to be known.[1]

'Martyr' has, both in Arabic and in Greek, two meanings: witnessing and dying in sacrifice. *Shahid* is the martyr, *Shahada* is to witness, to see. The gaze of the witness, reading the pain of others, the voyeuristic gaze may be more important, more thought after than the act itself. Obviously Sanaa could not see the blood, her own blood as she described it. None of the martyrs whose pictures were plastered over the walls of Beirut during the war did either. They did not exist any longer. Only their pictures, taken while they were alive, when they posed in a photography studio, were left for a while, for the passers-by to see, to witness. Witness as in the other meaning of the Greek word *martur*.

A very poignant and powerful image has been taken and exhibited by Joel Jabbour, a Palestinian artist of the family of a martyr. They seem to be looking for us, calling on us to witness their loss.

The dignity of the family is tragic and humbling. The dead son looks out at us from his portrait. His gaze is that of the martyr and the witness.

In the age of photography, martyrs come and go at a faster rate, as far as the visual memory is concerned. From the age of painting to the age of posters, the iconography of 'the beautiful martyr' has moved from Michelangelo to Andy Warhol. And from Warhol, through an

---

1.   Selection from a popular book in Arabic entitled *The Martyr in Islam*

ironic trick of the multiplied image, we are transported back into the age of Byzantine icons or faded and layered walls like the ones you see in the cathedral of the Annunciation in the Kremlin painted by Andrei Roublev or in some abandoned Orthodox Eastern churches. Let me speak through images.

The martyr is sometimes celebrated on his/her own, but often, multiplied. The space on the walls gets narrower and the martyrs compete for the space.

If it took a few hundred years for the walls of temples and churches to build up layers of painted images of saints and martyred believers; in our age, in the time I lived in war-torn Beirut, it took only a few days for the posters to turn the walls into an archaeological site. Today, in the age of Photoshop and the digital camera, the rate of poster proliferation, the making of rapid myths, makes Walter Benjamin's prediction seem archaic.

I cannot deny that these walls may have the beauty of layered walls in old temples, but this beauty is tragic. Listen to Mahmoud Abu Hashhash telling us about the walls in Palestine, another country close to mine that is suffocating under the threat of living posthumously:

> There is always space for one more poster on the walls of Palestinian towns. Yet if the walls are overcrowded with other posters, the new can always find a place on top of an older one. To strip the many layers of posters on a wall is to carry out a form of archaeology.[1]

I say tragic not only because of death and loss of life, but because the young men, and more recently women, have been cheated of their wish to be singled out, to see their picture shining on the wall like those of the stars (stars as in singers and actors and famous screen sirens). I don't know if I should feel sad for the seventeen-year-old Sanaa. She is now one, just one, of many women who have been celebrated as martyrs; there are so many 'suicide martyrs' nowadays, women

---

1.   *Poetics and Politics in the Visual Representation of Martyrdom in Palestine*, 2004

included, that the celebrations are frequent and more common; they last for a shorter time; they are quickly forgotten. The duality of extreme living and nihilism that turns people (usually young people) into wishful martyrs is reflected in the juxtaposition of the posters of martyrs and entertainers. The erasing of the image of one martyr to paste another on the wall is as rapid as the replacement of advertising boards announcing a concert or a dance performance by a famous belly dancer or a popular blockbuster film.

I do feel sad for these young men and women who went to the photographer's studio wishing to see their picture enlarged and plastered on the walls of the city like the pictures of their TV idols or the famous stars they admire.

Mahmoud Abu Hashhash writes:

In Palestine the photographer usually asks his client to go up to the photography cabinet, where there is a mirror and a comb to get ready for the camera. Next to the mirror there is a bell. The client should ring it when ready to be photographed, and the photographer comes in.

'What do you need the photo for?' asks the photographer.

'For a Palestinian passport,' an enthusiastic student who wants to study abroad may answer.

'For an American visa,' another one may answer with a smile.

'For an ID,' a boy may answer with the happiness of becoming a man.

'To send to my exiled son,' an elderly village woman may say.

'For the immigration application form,' a desperate young man may answer.

'To renew my Jordanian passport,' a man with a moustache would answer.

'I want a beautiful photograph to send to my fiancé in prison,' a young woman may answer shyly.

'I don't know,' another one may say.

The photographer sets up a suitable backdrop for the photograph. He then tries to straighten the client's head. He starts counting to three as a signal for the client to put a smile on his face. The client may or may not smile. But he will end up with at least one photograph. He looks at it; he may like or dislike it. He may go on to complete a formal procedure, or might tear it up once he steps out of the studio. He may put it in his wallet if it is small enough to fit, but he will never know that this exact photograph might one day be part of the public space after the necessary collage and manipulations for public exhibition have been made.

When I was a child my grandmother took me to the movies to see *The Passion of Christ*. The image of Christ crucified on the screen revealed to me my grandmother in a doubly embarrassing state: she was excited, enamoured with Christ played by Jeffrey Hunter; she was indulging in his suffering, had seen the movie more than once before she decided to take me with her, to turn me into a witness. And yet when it came time for Christ to be crucified and left to die on the cross my grandmother started screaming loudly, 'Christ, my dear Jesus, show them who you are, perform a miracle, walk away from this cross. Are you crazy? Why don't you kill these murderers?'

It was my first experience of the power of the body in pain and the aesthetic of its representation. It was the first time I saw a member of my family indulge in the images of pain, embarrassing me in public. A few years ago, I happened to be in Mexico on Good Friday, and I watched families grieving over replicas of sculptures of Christ crucified. The obvious thick red paint that stuck to the statue of Jesus did not deter any of the members of the families from weeping as if the crucified was their own son, father or brother. I have to admit that the red paint was so blunt, so obvious, that I failed to experience the sublime beauty of pain. The faces of the worshippers, on the other hand, mesmerized me, and their sorrow had beauty and power. I can only repeat after Picasso: 'Art is a lie that always says the Truth.'

The aesthetic of the body in pain, of the martyred hero, is similar in many ways across cultures and times. The abandoned passive body of Jesus Christ depicted in the famous Pietá is similar in posture, in the hanging of the arm to the side, to David's depiction of the death of Marat during the French Revolution and to many posters conceived for political consumption in the Middle East today.

I find the Mikhail Haddad image very puzzling. It is a Pietá, but the father replaces the weeping mother. Still the Palestinian martyr is also a body that is absolutely offered, abandoned.

I had to live through a bloody and violent civil war; I had to block out for years its concrete realities before I could think about the aesthetic of the body in pain. For a long time I couldn't even look again at Goya's etchings of the Disasters of War, let alone face the question of beauty and pain. For, believe me, when you experience cruelty and pain, when you are still carrying the smell, the odour of pain (and as I said images don't carry smells), when you have seen or felt the body in pain you cannot be a truthful witness: Rustom Barucha tells a story in the second issue of the journal of the Prince Claus Fund that I will always identify with.

In his article, 'Beauty in Context', he tells us about the Vietnamese playwright Le Thi Diem and her very painful story. In the course of a multicultural theatre conference she read her literary evocation of this pain. It was unanimously acknowledged that her writing was beautiful. Beauty-full. But the participants complained that she did not put more of herself into her story. She seemed 'very detached' from her pain. Pressurised by the participants desire for honesty, she confronted them with anger.

'I keep hearing,' she said, 'you write so beautifully. Do you know why I write so beautifully? It's because I don't want to tell the truth.'

For pain in reality is tough and horrible: images, words are after all mere representations. The representations are the lie that confirms the truth.

Before pain, before the real blood, images of promised heroism and sacrifice are bright and colourful. Look at the images of popular posters in Iran. The popular iconography is calling for mobilisation during a period of revolution and war.

Representation in large format posters of war and heroism hanging on the streets depict blood in its most radiant red. Grenades are offered by children like plates of pomegranates.

These images may be pure kitsch, but they did inflame the imagination of young men searching for a way out of the colourless future ahead of them. 'Life has become the ideology of its absence,' says Adorno.

The body actively in pain is an act that is performed during Ashura, when thousands of people self-inflict pain to share the ordeal of al-Hussein, the martyred son of Imam Ali. Here the blood is real. The images can be distressing. The rituals have fascinated many photographers and cultural analysts. Ashura is a commemoration and identification with the suffering of al-Hussein, the grandson of the Prophet Muhammad, killed by the Umayyad during the battle of Kerbala in 680. The Ashura mourning rituals have been performed for centuries, gaining a new momentum in the last few years in Iraq and in the south of Lebanon. In these yearly rituals it is the human condition and its suffering that is expressed. They are the closest thing to a passion play in which many actors are involved.

To speak of beauty here is disturbing, but how can we avoid the question? Peter Brook wrote in this context: 'I saw in a remote Iranian village one of the strongest things I have ever seen in theatre.' Beauty can be extracted and abstracted. Look at a few images of Ashura, of bodies in real and experienced pain taken by Gaith Abdul-ahad, an Iraqi photo-journalist, and then the aesthetised fragments enlarged by Jalal Toufic, an artist from Lebanon who has written many books on blood and its rituals. I am asking, screaming: Can we human beings abstract pain through beauty? Do we need to witness pain, even our own, in order to create beauty? Or are we creating beauty in order to exorcise pain?

The smell of blood during Ashura cannot be rendered by photographs and images. It is overwhelming in its silence.

I often wonder when I visit a Brit Art exhibition where morbidity, butchered cows and dung or sculptures made of real human blood are displayed how come the smell is absent. Do the artists and curators, as well as the visitors, dare only defy visual taboos? How come there are new major installations exploring the shock of body fluids, of skinned anatomies, or even of sound, but rarely any exploring the taboos of stench and the reaction to it?

Before I leave you with these questions I'll approach smell and beauty from a different angle. A story of pain and the image related to it; a touching story, an image of beauty that is no less dramatic than the images discussed earlier, but that speaks of an aroma of simple earthly pleasures:

Jean Paul Kaufman was kidnapped in Lebanon in the mid-eighties. He was kept for months chained and in solitary confinement in a dark narrow basement with nothing to help him forget about the long stagnant and miserable hours. Once, his jailers threw him a packet of processed cheese. He ate the cheese and kept the wrapping. He looked at the drawing on the cover of the box. A cow was painted over a background of kitsch blue sky and shiny green mountains.

The illustrator wanted to incite the consumers to think of fresh milk and natural dairy products. But Kaufman, despite his pained body and his desperate anguish, looked at the image and dreamt of his French countryside, his vineyards. These simple images triggered a memory of harvests and vintage wine. The beauty is in the smell, that of red wine and not that of blood; that of imagination that creates a reality seeking life and simple pleasures. An unknown illustrator that we hardly call an artist today had created an image that carried a wonderful smell on its surface. He had drawn an aromatic image. Is it beautiful?

Jamila is My Name

Look at me, look how pretty I am. Oh, you don't mind me combing my hair while we're speaking, do you? My hair has always been soft and silky. This is because I take good care of it; I comb it many times every day. Nothing comes easily, you know (*pour être belle il faut souffrir*). I love long hair, touching it, feeling its gentleness is so relaxing. I feel naked without make-up.

You don't mind me adjusting my eyeliner while we're chatting, do you?

Yes, you may say that I'm hiding behind my false eyelashes, my thick foundation and my red lipstick. I'm not denying that I escape my unease behind my make-up. Why does it bother you? Maybe not you in particular, but everybody else.

I've always had a girlish face. My body is really that of a woman, my breasts are suppressed in my flat chest, I dream of them bursting out of my tight skin. One day I'll have the body that suits my feeling about myself.

Would you like to listen to my story? I came here a few years ago, leaving behind the family that I miss so much. It hurts when I remember my mother; she's had no news about my whereabouts since the day I ran away. I wanted to spare her the agony of finding out that I would rather be her daughter than the son she proudly named Jamil.

My adolescence was lived in anguish and torment. I kept longing to be the child who lived among his mother's friends, among their skirts and linens, their perfumes and body creams. It smelled smooth, warm among women. Then I was kicked out of this paradise, sent among the men and their dark boring suits. I hated the hair that started to grow on my face and all over my chest. God, did I hate myself then.

I was so confused: a male body with a girl's face, a male body with a female identity. I felt angry at my mother for abandoning me and sending me away from her feminine world. I felt guilty for not wanting to be a man among the men.

I came to Beirut, where nobody knew me. This is how I became Jamila, a cabaret dancer. I gave the men the frisson of excitement that took hold of me each time I moved my round hips. My belly swirled like a snake under its discreet netting, my toes glittered with dark red polished nails and my legs were fabulous under the smooth silk stockings that the opening of my skirt revealed to desiring eyes.

I forgot about my pain and my confusion. I felt at peace with myself in the cabaret. I felt at home feeding the lustrous imagination of my audience, until the day when he showed up and he fell in love with me and I with him.

I don't want to lose him. I want to become entirely woman for him; I want to acquire the body that should have been mine.

Who feels like laughing at my plight?

On Kipling

Why am I so indulgent towards good artists? Rudyard Kipling is a great artist. A sculptor of words and, above all, a storyteller. He should have annoyed me with his Boy Scout mentality and his folkloric narrative. But no, despite his clichés and prejudices and primitive notions of manhood, I enjoy reading him. Imagination is not to be judged. That's what I say to myself. Deeds, yes! Celine gave us wonderful books, books full of offensive ideas, books that should nonetheless never have been banned.

But how unfair my comparisons are to Kipling. He never did anything; he simply wrote about *sahibs* and 'natives' as if he knew to which category he belonged, as if he had no identity issues of his own. Well, he did! And look at his dialogues. Isn't he one of the first to have written in phonetics, onomatopoeia-ing working-class accents, 'pidgin' English (*Petit-Negre* is what the little, run-of-the-mill mild-to-less-mild French racist would call it). Didn't Alice Walker in her *The Color Purple* do the same with black voices and sounds? Yes, but she is black. So are we reading a text or looking at the author's skin?

I do not find Kipling offensive. I am offended by those who are dangerous or threatening. Dangerous and threatening he is not. Great writer he often is. And let people express their prejudices. Who cares. I feel confident enough not to care, confident enough to judge the syntax for its own sake. No mature person can take his patronising seriously. And sometimes, maybe often, he has some nice tales to tell.

I cannot help it, but I need to profit from this space and direct my insults at Michel Houellebecq, while I am praising the literature of Kipling.

Houellebecq is a lousy writer; he is vicious in his declarations, trying his artificial best at being offensive. Playing at being a breaker of taboos; but his taboos are very carefully selected.

Kipling is not trying to offend; he is expressing himself, his own self with his own prejudices, contradictions and complexes. Fair play! Exotic settings? For whom? And so what? We all have our own exotic fantasies and they are not always politically correct. I may be saying the wrong thing, but my love for stories is limitless. Remember, his are stories, not facts.

On Choukri

'Choukri, hey Choukri!' is a sound you hear all the time when Mohammad Choukri takes you through the streets of Tangier. The caller could be a French filmmaker, an world-famous novelist or a woman cleaning the doorstep of a restaurant. They will all kiss this small, thin man whose name has become synonymous with Tangier, reflecting its endless contradictions. Choukri talks to the prostitutes and beggars who salute him on the streets in the same hospitable voice he uses to address the rich and famous film stars who've adopted this city as their home. He is the same energetic and nervous body whether he's in Café de France or on the concrete floor of a poor old acquaintance. From rags to riches without ever becoming rich, nobody lived Tangier, the city of sleaze and dreams, the cosmopolitan Afro-Mediterranean town, as deeply and intensely as Choukri did.

Choukri was illiterate until the age of twenty-one. A streetwise kid, he didn't escape any 'bad doing' or any of the pain kids like him – growing up at the bottom of the social scale – witness and endure. When he told his story in *For Bread Alone* people spoke of the

Moroccan Genet, of the most poignant Arab memoir ever written ... His blunt account of life as a kid on the streets, selling anything, including himself, to survive, insulting the god that made human beings suffer like him and his brother (his brother died in front of him at the hands of his angry father), was not to please the censors. It's hardly surprising that this bestselling book, published in at least thirteen languages, was banned in his country of origin when it first appeared.

Thanks to his friend, Mohammad Barrada, then head of the Moroccan Union of Writers, a direct contact was established between Choukri and Beirut/London-based publishers, Saqi. Saqi decided to defy the censors in the Arab world and publish Choukri's autobiography, as it first appeared in all its blunt and cruel truth, in its terrible spontaneity. This was 1986. Unsurprisingly, the book was banned in many Arab countries, but, for the same reason, it was smuggled incessantly and profusely by readers to all these countries.

Choukri learned to read and write as a grown man. He pulled himself out of the gutter of misery. He was sought after and befriended by many great and famous writers like Tennessee Williams, Jean Genet, Paul Bowles. But Choukri never tried to garner fame from their company. The source of his pride was the fact that he had become a teacher, and that he presented a literary programme on the radio. *I am not only literate*, he seemed to affirm, *but I am also cultured*. At no stage did the cultured Choukri betray his life story. In his autobiographical novel *Streetwise* he tells of his addictions and his days in a mental asylum following an outburst of violence that he had not yet learned to tame. His courage and his warmth made no concession to fame, or to his now internationally acclaimed image. Mohammad Choukri hardly ever left Tangier; he found it difficult to breathe a different air.

When I last visited Choukri he was very thin, and getting thinner by the day. Choukri never ate; he drank. I'll never forget one strange incident. One evening, walking me back to my hotel, he suddenly stopped and said, 'On the corner of this street is the café of the intellectuals. You cannot visit Tangier without going there.' I was exhausted, but couldn't miss such an opportunity. Once inside, I saw faces that looked like they were more under the influence of alcohol than books. I saw women who hadn't bothered to adjust their unbuttoned shirts. The place was ethereal and relaxed, lit by a dim red light. Choukri knew every man and woman in this café. He insisted on walking me back to my hotel later, much later, that night.

The following day, on our way to a meeting to discuss his new book, we passed this same café.

'Look,' I said, 'that's where we were yesterday!'

He looked at me bewildered and said, 'You should never go into places like that. Who took you there?'

Choukri wrote and debated literature with the intellectuals who visited him regularly, and he drank in the familiar bars of Tangier, where he met his old friends, the poor and the unemployed as well as the women who had nothing to offer but their bodies. He treated his less lucky friends with such respect that you could only admire him. He was an authentic person in the best sense of the word: authentic as in real and not as in pure. Purity or harmony is not what Tangier is about; its cafés and nightclubs are as noisy as the scratched speakers of the muezzins calling the believers – in a non-synchronised way – to prayer. Choukri didn't respond to the muezzin's call, but nobody responded to the Islamic duty of *zakat* as he did: he never failed to stop near a beggar – and there are many beggars on the streets of Tangier – to share what little he had, chatting with the ones he knew personally. Walking with Choukri in Tangier takes longer for he's always stopping and greeting friends or chatting to strangers who recognise this famous writer. Tangier will never be the same without the sound of someone calling, 'Choukri, hey Choukri!'

Reading a Book by Its Cover

My colleague André Gaspard and I came to London in the late 1970s, fleeing the civil war in Beirut. We were total strangers to this city. We were such newcomers that when we started Al Saqi Books we mailed our first catalogue to addresses in the telephone book. We stayed up whole nights looking through the directories, trying to find names that sounded like potential readers for our books. When I remember those days, I realise how eager and hard-working immigrants often are, for they have to start from zero. They have to build on an empty base and this is why – I hope this is also true in our case – they may build more creatively.

Once the catalogues were sent, we waited and panicked. You can imagine our great joy when a librarian from the Oriental section of Cambridge University Library showed up in our bookshop, holding the catalogue in one hand and selecting all the novels of Neguib Mahfouz with the other. The novels were obviously in Arabic, for in 1979 Mahfouz hadn't been widely translated into English.

A few weeks later the same librarian called us and in a hesitant voice, interrupted by many embarrassed coughs, asked, 'Uh, eh, is there any chance you could provide me with some different editions of Mahfouz's novels? Nobody reads Arabic in the acquisitions department and they all think that I'm ordering, uh, uh, pornographic books or erotica!'

We rushed back to our shelves, looked at the only edition of Mahfouz's novels available, and smiled. These covers have been with us since the fifties and it never crossed our minds that the images could be considered sexy by anyone. These were the popular images exhibited all over Cairo, Beirut or Damascus as posters for the films based on Mahfouz's or Abdel Qudous's novels.

Since that day I've become enamoured with the subject of book covers.

Can you read an Arabic book by its cover?

You *can* read a book by its cover, say the English.

L'habit ne fait pas le moine, say the French.

The Arabs, who have always privileged the Word, say *Yuqra' al Maktub min Inwanihi*, you can read the written from its title.

It's tempting to believe the French. But this is too easy, too hasty. A cover is a façade and a façade reveals as much as it hides. The façade of a building protects the intimacy of its inhabitants, but it also reveals many of their customs and attitudes through the width of its windows, its balconies and the laundry hanging outside or hidden from others' eyes.

The covers of Mahfouz and Abdelqudous speak a lot about ours and our society's image of itself – for fashion, like façades or covers, is the bearer of our traditions as well as our transgression of these traditions; it is also the bearer of our impulses and imagined selves.

If we study these pictures they will tell us about the image of the ideal or attractive woman in the popular iconography: white, blonde. These images speak of the subconsciously accepted equation that Western equals fairer equals more beautiful. Somehow most men look Oriental in these pictures; they are either darker, moustached or dressed in a traditional Egyptian peasant hat, while the women are all inspired by Anita Ekberg or Gina Lollobrigida or some other Hollywood sex symbol.

These, as far as I know, are not at all central to Mahfouz's socially oriented literature. On the other hand the constant tension between modernity and tradition is revealed by the sophisticated blonde lady versus the covered peasant, both desirable in their own way, both competing for the minds and hearts of Arabs and their vision of their society's future.

You cannot read an Arabic book by its cover then?

Well! Let us consider Cairo today, where most billboards are for Islamic fashion boutiques, with veiled models advertising the latest headscarf or the latest in Islamic sportswear. I guess that these covers, stretched all over the pavements and in news-stands speak of the continuous cohabitation of opposite tendencies and dreams or future visions of Egyptian society and, for that matter, of many Arab societies.

Now in a domain and in an area where censorship is still the norm, the cover or the façade can be a good way to trick the censor. Many people used to replace the cover with a respectable (consensual) one before sending a book by mail. Many dissident or religiously incorrect books have been sent across borders thanks to new binding carrying titles like *Studies in Medical Surgery* or some such. Nobody can really ban ideas. Censors can only make life more miserable for people, or momentarily narrow and impoverish people's intellectual life or freedom of choice. They can deprive the poorest, those who are most isolated, less travelled and with least access to private satellite dishes from first-hand access to widely spread knowledge or facts and images. For me the impoverishment is summarised by the question many visitors to London ask as soon as they visit Saqi: 'Where is the section of banned books?' Obviously there is no such section in any library or bookshop, but the deprived is like an addict; he or she doesn't have the luxury to select and choose.

I remember that when I was in high school our French teacher ridiculed a fellow student because she had catalogued Baudelaire's *Les Fleurs du Mal* under 'Botanical' in the school library. I still feel bad about our spiteful laughter; obviously this young student couldn't have guessed the content of the book by its cover.

I once experienced the opposite phenomenon – that is when a book is too obviously read through its cover. I had been asked many times about the original Arabic edition of Sheikh Nefzawi's *The Perfumed Garden*. This book is widely exhibited and sold on the streets of Morocco but banned, in principle, in the Middle East. I was told about the bookseller who had printed it in the early 1970s in Beirut, so I went there and found his son in charge of the business. When I asked the son about Nefzawi's book, he asked me to be discreet and admitted having many copies in stock. But he insisted that 'a lady like you' should not read this book. He was quite satisfied with my answer. 'Don't worry,' I said, 'I sell books, I don't read them!' When I saw the book I felt that my answer should have been, 'I sell books, I don't look at their covers.' The cover bore a rough cutting of a 1960s American model carrying a tray. The publisher had replaced the commodity advertised on the tray with a penis.

Why did this man's father have to print such covers? He wanted to sex up his book, but he ended up in jail for a few days because of his artistic entrepreneurial spirit. Why did he not continue the old Arabic tradition of book covers – leather or simili leather cover with abstract Islamic patterns and calligraphy, generally embossed in gold? After all, great classic writers like Suyuti managed well a few centuries ago with their books (ranging from explanations of the *Qur'an* to manuals for better sexual performance) printed behind the same Islamic abstract cover designs.

Sometimes it is better not to read a book by its cover

A fascination with book covers as cultural vitrines, as Western versus Oriental imagery, led me with another artist, Shaheen Merali, to explore the issue of identity, of globalisation, our reality as New Europeans through the art of book covers. Two years ago we embarked on an art project, an installation called *Dressing-Readdressing*. This touring exhibition, starting in London and finishing in Beirut via Vancouver, consisted of manipulating book covers. Through collage we tarbooshed (put on a fez) and veiled figures on classical English books and we westernised the covers of Arabic books.

Can we change the identity, the content of a book through its cover? Are identities inherited or are they constantly shifting?

Covers, façades, dress are important. Some believe that they do influence attitudes and behaviour. National leaders often believe in the symbolic power of dress. Ataturk banned the fez from men's heads as he was seriously convinced that modernity and the red *couvre-chef* were incompatible! Hoda Shaarawi, the founder of the Egyptian women's movement, took off her veil only after her husband's death. Today in France, many young female Beurs are challenging the French educational authorities as well as their parents and claiming their '*droit a la difference*' by choosing to cover their head with an Islamic hijab.

In Beirut we went through the opposite process, dressing Arab covers in western styles, and we realised that identity and authenticity are even more constructed than the discourse about them reveals. Putting a tie on an Arab or Indian man, putting a 'cool' T-shirt on a Bedouin woman, triggered no surprise or clash to the eyes. Globalisation is in effect mostly westernization. In order to create a dichotomy, a discrepancy, we had to put our characters to work. King Farouk was already wearing a tie under his tarboosh, so we turned him into a health freak, sweating in the gym. Arab tribesmen can easily exchange their tribal solidarity for that of a football team. The uniformity imposed by the veil on women is not far from the uniformity of the famished models selling the latest designer clothes.

In our world of exchanged identities and swiftly travelling images, it is more and more difficult to read a book by its cover, and maybe this is a blessing, maybe this will make us all less prejudiced.

Soft Round Suzy

Believe me, I'm not obsessed with identity, belonging and cultural clashes. I'm fed up with the volumes that have tried to explore the 'problem of roots'. But of all the places (I mean actual physical space and not a paradigmic cultural space where I could have been made to face the question of identity) it was The Studio, where my Oriental dance classes took place, which brought me face to face with this unavoidable and dominant issue that has bored the hell out of our century. Don't laugh; I'm serious! Bear with me for a few moments and then you can judge me, believe me or laugh at me.

The Studio is the professional dance centre where Samara (original name Janet) teaches Arabic/Oriental dance. Why did I go there in the first place? Definitely not to connect with my cultural roots, near Piccadilly Circus, in the middle of cold and rainy London. Not at all! I went there for fun, in order to dance and dance a bit better than I spontaneously knew how to. Or so I believed. Actually, to be honest, I had been to a previous course, given in a women's centre in the Regent's Park area, but that was short-lived. The centre, encouraged by some radical feminist – the type that existed for a while in the 1980s – kicked us all out. This dance, wrongly called belly dance when most of its undulations come from the neck and the arms, or the shoulders and the hips, didn't strike them as a big contribution to the struggle against male oppression. And despite the fact that the class was composed entirely of female members, the teacher brought her baby boy with her, and boys, not even the animal kind, were allowed in the centre.

So here we were in The Studio, moving to the rhythm of Sufi drummers and undulating with the melodies of Mohammed Abdel-Wahab, while next door the classical ballet class endlessly repeated Tchaikovsky's *Swan Lake* to some dozen famished young women trying desperately to stretch their legs in totally opposite and impossible directions.

What does the problem of identity have to do with all this chatter, you may ask. I did ask for your patience, didn't I?

Well, it all has to do with Suzy: white, creamy, sweet Suzy. She was the awkward girl who chose the furthest corner of the dance studio, and who removed herself as much as possible from the front mirror. I'll never forget the first time Suzy stepped into The Studio. Shy and round, her body closed in on itself and her face seemed more interested in the floor than the space above it. Clumsy, graceless Suzy, who despite being in her late twenties, looked more like an unhappy teenager whose only consolation in life was chocolate or fatty sweets kept in abundance in her handbag. Suzy passed by the next-door class, with its tortured skeletal dancers, like a woman on the run. Not even a quick glance! As if she couldn't bear the thought that some women – her own age – could be stretched up so high while she had to crouch in and low. Suzy had big brown eyes, but you hardly ever saw them for they avoided you as much as they did the ten-metre-long mirror that imposed itself on all of us and on our little egos.

Poor unhappy, uneasy Suzy. Not for long though, not for very long. It took two lessons, two one-hour classes for Suzy to be transformed. Was it our envying gaze that gave her the self-confidence to become the star of Arabic dance among us mediocre performers? Suzy's ample chest and wide full hips served perfectly well the curves and the shimmers that the music required. All of us – and Josephine, who'd joined us from the ballet class next door, more than anyone – kept getting out of breath, eagerly twisting our waists to emphasise our floating curves. Josephine was a desolate portrait of angular and inadequate bones that no rolling could render sensual or even smooth. Suzy was suave and comfortable in her figures of eight; her shakes were subtle, for they appeared to be effortless. Her belly, round and full, followed the turn of her hips with proud and ample ease.

Beautiful Suzy. She now held her head high, her eyes were turning flirtatious, and we were all mesmerised.

Soon after her first success Suzy enhanced her brown gaze with generous kohl powder; she started wearing long elegant Oriental golden earrings that tinkled when she moved. She was never to part again from her colourful scarves knotted high and glamorously above her forehead. Suzy turned into an exotic and sexy Oriental woman. True, her colourless faded blond hair had been treated with dark black henna, but who remembers the original colour of her hair?

Look at Suzy now. She walks energetically, carrying her ample body with glamour and sensuality. Suzy smells of amber and musk and fills The Studio with glittering joy. Her presence conjures images from familiar paintings, when women had bellies and curves and their skin felt wonderfully smooth under the master's brush.

Suzy had discovered and created a new identity for herself.

Suzy carries incense and perfumes in her bag now, and brings almond cakes to class. Almond-flavoured sweets are a treat she discovered on her last visit to Morocco. She has invited us all, Josephine included, to an evening of dance and couscous at her home. Yes, there is a new and happy Suzy.

The real Suzy, the true one is born! The most eager travellers from Europe could never have dreamt of such an imagined Orient, and the

North African beauties painted by Delacroix could never have dreamt of looking more authentic and desirable.

I was the only Arab woman in the class, but Suzy looked and dressed like a real one. I have to admit the thought of finding a new identity for myself was tempting. I even considered some salsa lessons and Latino-style attitudes. But I didn't have the same courage Suzy had. She had reinvented her identity while I kept on, dragging behind me my weak and unassertive roots.

Red Lips

I was once involved in building an installation on the theme of refugees. One part of the installation consisted of objects that could be easily carried along if one had to leave home and venture into an unknown future with little or no advanced warning. The objects sent to the artists were mainly memories of survival: keys, deeds, diplomas, radios, purses. Only one item defied what seemed essential for a future of migration into the unknown – a tube of red lipstick. To me this did not seem like a light and superfluous item to take. I understood immediately the source of the sender's survival reflex. She – for it can only be a woman or a man who feels like a woman – was ready to journey along a dark road carrying a strong message of life and defiant energy. I understood because of the red lipstick marks that still haunt a corner of my memory, hidden like an explosive dream in a now-abandoned convent that once stood discreetly on a hill, high up in the Lebanese mountains.

I was a teenager preparing for the baccalaureate exam with my friends, Nada and Joumana, when we decided on a tranquil location that was ideal for concentration. Silence and a long distance from the city and its attractions became crucial for our studious goal. A secluded convent run by Italian nuns for novices seemed perfect: it removed us from the presence of males for two weeks. *Retraite* was the word we used in those days – retreating, withdrawing from ordinary life, from our routine, but mainly from the lightness of normal being.

The convent was hauntingly silent. We learned from a somewhat less rigorous Italian nun that the order was hosting very young girls from 'respectable families' whose fortunes had known better times and who, for lack of a dowry, were unmarriageable. A convent was the most suitable alternative for these would-be spinsters, especially this one, where only girls from *bonnes familles* were admitted. The deadly silence that surrounded us was eerie, thanks to the binding oath made by every newcomer ('privileged girls', as our nun put it) to remain mute for six months. The few Italian nuns who ran the place spoke as little and as softly as possible, out of respect for the novices' vow and out of love for 'the tears of Mary and the suffering of her son, Jesus Christ'.

There were tens of novices, rushing silently through the dark corridors. We met them briefly on our way to the dining room, and our curious eyes searched eagerly for their faces, but they always managed to escape our gaze. Their eyes avoided us, fixing incessantly on the tiled floor whenever they passed us. Their bodies looked small and fragile under their neat black tunics. Only the Mother Superior appeared tall and upright in this convent. Her instructions, on the first day of our retreat, were uttered through thin lips that were as stiff as the rules that presided over the lives of this community of secluded and hushed women.

We were scheduled to spend two weeks in this haven of perfect isolation, but on the seventh day the scene that recurs like a dark red dream in my sleepless nights turned the convent into disarray, cutting short our worthy and scholarly endeavour. It is because of this scene, on the seventh day in this remote convent, that I understand how a refugee can proudly hold a lipstick tube in the face of a threatening future.

Red is the Absolute: it is pure. Its dazzling power stands for the warmth of the sun and the mystery of life. Red is transgression. Red is energy.

The Mother Superior's lips loosened into a delighted smile when she informed us that today was the pope's feast day and that the novices would be allowed to roam freely around the convent, to enjoy themselves any way they saw fit as long as the vow of silence was respected. Soon a few novices stood near the door of the large room that Nada, Joumana and I were sharing. Their steps, at first timid and hesitant, became more assertive upon our insistent hospitality. They were obviously amazed by our messy and overcrowded room, but their faces turned crimson and more candid when Nada produced a large tin full of biscuits. They suppressed their giggles, hiding their mouths with their hands, as Nada battled with layers of clothes and books, mingled with some make-up kits, to free a box packed with sweets and chocolates. A bullet-like stick fell out, rolling noisily onto the bare floor. Joumana picked it up and moved towards the mirror. She could never resist lipstick: she pulled off its golden cover, revealing a glittering magenta that she spread magnificently over her stretched lips.

Since ancient Egyptian times women have been staining their lips with everything from berry juice to henna, from a paste made of crushed red rocks to the combo of wax. The ancient Egyptians went to their graves with rouged lips.

I do not have a clear memory of how it all started. All I can see now is a room turned upside down by a bewildering frenzy. The novices were smearing their faces with all the lipstick the three of us had brought: they took hold of our make-up kits like famished birds of prey competing for their victims. They snatched them from each other, looking for more under the sheets, behind the books, under the tables. Red, cherry red, mulberry, burgundy paste everywhere, all over the novices' lips. Red like cranberry juice, like deep wounds. Graffiti red, dark orange patches over white skin and pale necks. Soon the novices started exchanging shades of red, rushing back and forth to the mirror, looking victoriously at their own reflection, tearing off their veils and collars, revealing shaved and patchy skulls, wiping off the spots they had kissed over and over again on the mirror to make new space for lip marks, for the fresh red stains on the mirror's surface.

Red is the colour of fire and blood. It is the fire that burns inside the individual. Below the green of the earth's surface and the blackness of the soil lies the redness, pre-eminently holy and secret. It is the colour of the soul, the libido and the heart. It is the colour of esoteric lore, forbidden to the uninitiated.

A novice, short and wilful-looking with her flushed baby face, went into wild, intoxicating motions. She kept bending her torso, throwing her shaved head downwards, springing her body upright and flinging her arms in all directions. She seemed to perform an angry and disconnected ritualised dance, oblivious to the uproar and chaos surrounding her. Noises emerged from the red faces that twirled and rushed around, filling the room with a buzzing sound. Sounds like shrieking laughter came out of red candy throats and brown glittering tongues. Screams like those of warriors seeking a desperate victory emerged from the now-exposed and shaved heads of the frantic novices. Some had patches of hair scattered over their skull like badly tended lawns. I suddenly realised that more novices had joined in the frenzied feast, turning our room into a frightening maze of violet and wine-dark surfaces.

Red embodies the ardour and enthusiasm of youth. It is the colour of blood, the heat of the temper. It gives energy to excitement and to inflamed physical conditions. With its warlike symbolism, red will always be the spoils of war or of the dialectic between heaven and earth. It is the colour of Dionysus, the liberator and orgiastic.

The tall, dark figure of the Mother Superior loomed before us, putting a sudden end to the uncontrollable madness in the room. She must have been standing there, unnoticed, for a while before silence fell, which now looked like an abandoned and desolate battlefield. It was a heavy and long silence that emphasised the languid embrace of two novices oblivious to the sudden change of mood around them. With her eyes half closed, and her head leaning against the wall, one of the two was lustfully offering her neck, smeared with red lip marks, to the passionate kisses of the other.

Rage like red burning arrows tensed the lips of the Mother Superior, intensifying the paleness of her complexion. She appeared like a colourless mask strapped inside her black tunic, as rigid as a tightrope-walker immobilised in a snapshot.

'Stop it!' she finally managed to scream. Her cry had the effect of a slap hitting the two novices on the face. They disentangled their bodies furtively and rushed out of the room.

Red is the colour of the heart. Red is forbidden, free, impulsive. Red roses like the petals of desire. Did you know that in the 1700s the British Parliament passed a law condemning lipstick? It stated that women found guilty of seducing men into matrimony by cosmetic means could be tried for witchcraft. How was this law received in the red light district?

Her words resonated sharply in the silent room. She was like a general summoning a fallen army on a desolate and chaotic battlefield. The novice, who had been dancing and spinning like a drunken scarecrow, was now lying on the floor, smiling through her half-open lips – pink-purple lips – in a state of placid and satisfied detachment, while the Mother Superior stood like pure anger, controlled and obstinate.

Red is anger. Red warns, forbids and awakens vigilance. Red is blood, red is fire. Red like full-bodied wine is the devil's choice.

'Evil! Dirty! Evil!' The words emerged from the depth of her throat, as if struggling to get through her thin lips. 'The devil has conquered your souls and your flesh. The wombs of your mothers have rejected you and you have fallen into a dark abyss. Shame, shame on you and on your families! Ugly girls! Your lips are scarlet like the sinner's lips. Jesus will not be sacrificed twice. You will not be saved. Your bad blood has pierced your skin and stained your tunics. You will burn in hell, in deep red flames. Only fire will cleanse your swollen lips and spoiled innocence.'

The Mother Superior's tongue was moving fast, spinning like a wounded snake inside her wax-pale face. She was shaking but remained upright, stiff and furious, exhorting the forces of evil that had bewitched her novices.

'Go back to your rooms and lock yourselves in. You have wounded Jesus Christ and desecrated his home.'

Nocturnal red is the colour of the fire that burns within the individual and the earth. It is the colour of the devil's laughter, of hell's flames. Red is revolt.

There was a war and the convent is no longer there. It is said that two of the novices stayed behind in a rented brick house not far from the abandoned convent. According to the villagers they live like hermits, except that their lips are always heavily painted with bright red lipstick.

Janis Joplin

Hey, Janis, tell me what is it you're singing? What are you screaming out of your soul, out of your body and your pain? The blues? Soul? Pop? Rebellion? Tell me! Forget about this damn bottle of Southern Comfort that never leaves you and tell me. But no, don't say a thing, just do what you know how to do like a goddess: sing. Sing louder. Sing harder.

Transcend your vocal cords. Wage war against limits! *Why, Why, Why? It ain't fair, this can't be* you cry in front of a worshipping crowd. And I repeat why, why, why did you have to work for your death as if it was imperative, as if you were rushing towards your own execution. You still had a lot to give; you were still so young. You could have tried a little bit harder; you could have tried to stick around a little longer. Janis, your tragedy is that of the sixties, Janis the star, the woman, the rebel, the girl who transcended pain by confronting it with intelligence, dignity, fun and art.

Hush. Don't explain! I know how difficult it must have been for you: growing up in the fifties, in Texas. Not the pretty and popular

Miss America girl. No. Not in the eyes and desires of white Middle America. You had acne, you weren't slim, and you suffered like many teenage girls who didn't fit in, ignored and humiliated.

'They laughed me out of class, they laughed me out of school and they laughed me out of town,' you declared bitterly.

The sixties were on the agenda; you went to California and you were one of its makers – creating a new beauty, inventing a liberated, daring, bewildered beauty. You emerged in your garish imaginative frocks. Hippie was the style, the images free, and we all dressed in multilayered, multicoloured attire. Even the girls who'd called you an ugly duckling in their provincial self-satisfaction wished they could look as exciting as you did.

Janis, your name is still written in big tragic letters, passionate like the dream of Martin Luther King, stormy like the speeches of Malcolm X. Your voice was powerful, vibrating through the demonstrations against the war in Vietnam. Poetic like the beat in Allen Ginsberg's verses.

Janis, you were gone with the sixties, you perished like this other great icon, Marilyn, the blonde dream who, like you, became addicted to being worshipped by the crowds. The craving killed her as it killed you. She had lost her war against limits, and so had you.

Painkiller, killer dope, damn you! You had the last word.

'On stage I make love to twenty-five thousand people, then I go home alone,' you once said.

On 4 October 1970 you went home alone singing drunkenly, 'I know you're gonna miss me, baby. You'll find that your life will be like mine, all wrapped up in a ball and chain.'

We are still here, listening to you and missing you.

Harrouda: A Tale of a Woman and Two Cities

Soon Harrouda will be thirty years old ... You'd have thought that she'd have grown bigger in my memory after all these years. But no, not only has she not aged at all and not put on a wrinkle on her face (*elle n'a pas pris une ride*) but she has become more monstrous, more revealing and her vagina more engulfing.

When Harrouda first appeared to me in the form of words, poems and tales, I must have been too young. She fascinated and frightened me, as do women who are too large for our protected minds and our awkward imagination. Now, going through its pages for the second time, now that I am less naïve and more ambiguous, I can better understand her multiple discourse. To use the language of her son and creator Taher Ben Jalloun, I can inhale better the smells exhumed through the virtues and sins of her flesh. Here is a woman, a symbol that easily rivals Fellini's outrageous creations, that speaks for Bataille's sensual morbidity and takes hold of two cities in Morocco, Fez and Tangier. Harrouda is nonetheless totally secure in her identities: she is African, she speaks Arabic and prays for the Muslim prophet, and when men in authority are not looking she prays to Moulay Idriss. She is mother and lover; she is as real as our wild fantasies.

'Harrouda' is a poem where the masculine and the feminine look each other straight in the eye, fighting unequally for their space and giving the Muslim cities their omnipresent sexual tension. There is a moist sensuality in this 'reading in the body'. Not a sweet kind of sensuality, the kitschy refined one that is displayed on exotic travel magazines and leaflets. The sensuality of Harrouda, woman, symbol and nightmare, is that of 'the real pleasure of a slaughtered flesh', a pleasure that is found in the demonic invitation of her thighs, in her lost and regained innocence. She tells the young men that they are all her children and that they can sleep between her legs. You can read 'Harrouda' however you wish, with your eyes overlooking the words and your fingers on its pages, or you can read it in a deviant manner, for Ben Jalloun warns us in his wonderful French that *'Seule une lecture déviée est reelle'*.

Taher Ben Jalloun writes like a narrator on stage, appearing and disappearing incessantly through the chink in a thick curtain. A rich, thick curtain made of silk and rough jute. A talented storyteller will allow millions of stories and realities to escape through those little openings in the curtain. And our storyteller *is* talented. He spins his stories and tales like only a man who has visited many cultures and looked deeply into many civilisations can do – travelling from Fez ('Fass', as its people pronounce it and the author likes spelling it) to Tangier, from tradition and 'virtue' to glitter and 'treason'. But things are never as simple as that, for it is in 'Fass' that the old teacher taught the boys how to read the holy book while they dreamt with blasphemous sarcasm. If Tangier is the city where Genet and Burroughs landed, seeking darkness and pleasure, it is at the same time a space that the big screen has shaped and influenced. Is Tangier imitating its screen image or is the cinema reproducing its reality? Ben Jalloun was asking this question long before the postmoderns started debating the subjectivity of 'concrete facts' and the lost space between image and reality.

And Fass; Fass, the learned and virtuous, do we realise when we look on with wonder at its artisanal products that its artisans have been despised by the rulers of a city, of a culture that venerates the Word?

A kind of malaise takes hold of me, though, when the author speaks of the pleasure of humiliation that is given by the pretty young boys of Tangier to some of its visitors. Is he bothered by the unequal relations, the ugliness of prostitution? This is revolting in all kinds of relations; why insist on the rapport of the flesh in particular? But do not forget: Harrouda is flesh, lots of flesh, too big for the tanned and slender kids lying on the beaches of Tangier.

Very many things are unveiled while Harrouda is releasing her hair, coming out of a gutter or becoming invisible and saintly. Fez-Tangier, an itinerary of guilt and pleasure, pious words and less holy deeds. Harrouda travels on the crooked route and shapes it with her immensity.

Beirut and Contradiction:
Reading the World Press Photo Award

I am certain that Spencer Platt's picture, which won the World Press Photo Award for 2006, looked disturbing and even repellent to most viewers at first glance. I admit that it bothered me when I first saw it on my screen. But I also admit that I kept on looking at it. What was it that intrigued me in this picture despite my unexplained revulsion?

Why did I feel that I had to write about what I saw in the picture? It started with the reactions of others. I received the photo by email from a young Lebanese woman who commented, 'A prize for an American photo of Lebanon!' I guessed it meant there was something wrong, even some plot behind the photo and the prize.

My colleague, who heard me utter 'Good Lord' to my computer, came closer, had a quick look and said without a second's hesitation, 'This reminds me of *Rebel Without a Cause*.' You remember this cult movie, starring the young and beautiful James Dean? The red convertible car must have inspired his remark, along with the glamorous youth taking a ride inside it.

I said to myself, there is something bizarre in my colleague's remark, for it is not enough to see a fancy car and a few pretty faces to recall James Dean and Hollywood's cults. But after a moment's pause I realised that his reaction was not shallow: think cars, beautiful young people and ... think also of death, and you have a good reason to remember James Dean and his rebellion.

That same afternoon I went to a housewarming party and I overheard two young Lebanese arguing about the same photo. Both were in their twenties and very 'cosmopolitan'. One said: 'I think this is a great photograph. It shows us as we are, not people associated only with war and destruction.' The second one was appalled and said: 'This is the "new orientalism" – instead of the women depicted in Delacroix's classic orientalist paintings, today we have these modern, model-type Lebanese women against a background of war and poverty.'

The photo won the award on 9 February 2007 because, according to the jury, it shows Lebanon's contradictions. World Press Photo jury chair Michele McNally describes the winning image:

It's a picture you can keep looking at. It has the complexity and contradiction of real life, amidst chaos. This photograph makes you look beyond the obvious.

This is fair enough. The photo does show the contradictions of a country where destruction and the love of fun are unbearably juxtaposed, or mixed together to the point of exhaustion. The background is brown and grey, as it is in reality. Like a devastating tragedy of rubble mixed with the colours of lost interiors. The car is sparkling red, and the white T-shirt of the blonde woman in the car or the handkerchief covering the nose of the woman in the sleeveless black dress are whiter than the shirt of a passer-by going about his daily routine; the passer-by too, as well as the woman wearing the headscarf, are living in this destroyed neighbourhood. The driver of

the convertible car looks like a pop singer or a character from a recent *Star Academy* TV show. If the photographer had wanted to invent such contradictions, he could not have done better.

Still, if I had been a member of the jury, this is not the justification I would have given for the well-deserved prize. I believe that the photo is stunning in the metaphor it creates about war photography. It tells us about the voyeurism of the photographer, of the act of taking photos in tragic situations: if there is a contradiction, it is in the encounter between art, beauty and tragedy. Covering a disaster in order to create a striking image is what Robert Capa did best, he became an icon for it and we, the viewers, are becoming addicted to this art form.

Here is an image, a mirror of the self, an inverted gaze shot impulsively or in 'cold blood' by the photographer/artist. The act of taking a picture by the photographer Spencer Platt is mirrored and seen through the woman whose face is strained and body tilted while taking a picture of the same devastation from the seat of the red car. Did the photographer question his own behaviour by showing the voyeurism of another person, a non-professional? Is he saying that the voyeur's need to witness human misery and affliction, and to let others see it through their eyes, is in all of us?

Maybe the obvious reference to voyeurism is what triggered my first reaction, my rejection of a testimony that was offered to me before I had time to really look at it. Somehow, somewhere, the images of Helmut Newton came to mind – despite the fact that there is nothing erotic or pornographic in Platt's picture. Now I can see where I went wrong and got confused, how I needed to focus better to seize the allusion to voyeurism and the art of the camera that Newton shares with war photographers as they create images for the press.

Looking closely, the photo has nothing lurid in it: it is when art has to face human suffering and does not isolate tragedy from the ironies of survival that the absurdity of being hits us in the face.

Sawsan and the Devil

The women advanced in a noisy chaotic and confused procession.
Sawsan saw their excited faces advancing towards her. Some women
were raising their flutes, others walked behind their tambourines
and derboukas. The richest among them gave her a generous smile,
revealing a mouth proud of its numerous gold teeth, and the poorest
were tightening their grips on squawking chickens. The hysterical
birds, brought to be slaughtered during the ceremony, were tragically
resisting their fate.

Sawsan was terrified. What if they discovered her secret? What
would all these feverish faces do to her?

All she wanted was to force her husband to repudiate her. She'd
disliked him the moment she saw him. She'd tried to accept him but
instead she ended up hating him. She could hardly control her disgust
when he approached her. This is why she'd started mixing the herbs
that could pacify his seed in her womb, and for two years now it had
worked: she was still childless. She hadn't revealed her secret to a soul,
and she was determined to remain sterile until he took another wife

and rejected her. But instead, he took her from one doctor to another. Once, they travelled for three days and three long nights by bus to see the famous professor who had performed miracles on other barren wombs.

She doesn't remember when she overheard them saying that modern medicine couldn't cure her because she was 'possessed by the devil'. It was then that the women around her decided that unless the devil was chased out of her body she'd have no chance of giving her husband the son he longed for.

Here they were, all passion and fury, bursting with energy, releasing their frustrations into a frenzied dance and indulging in a ritual of hatred for the devil, who wouldn't let go of her womb.

They should never doubt her innocence, she'd be damned if her secret was revealed. She would give her body to the musicians' rhythms, to the *youyous* of the women and the thrill of the crowd. They needed to exorcise the devil, and she, who knew better, wanted to get rid of this husband of hers! She was angry, angry at her fate, angry at their excited red faces.

She extends her arms, loosens her muscles and starts whirling, slowly giving in to the repetitive beat of the drums and the lamenting chants of the flutes. She draws energy from the palms of her hands, channels it through her breasts, her hips, her thighs and then releases it with a shudder through her legs. The women around her start rotating their heads, first smoothly, then rapidly and frantically until their hair is spinning freely away from their bodies.

Her body plunges into a fight against gravity. Her body is freed from her own existence. She curls and quivers and spins out of reality. She enters into a frantic trance and screams: 'The branches of the forest are shivering vigorously for me; the thunder has scratched the sky with my anger.'

Sawsan is lying on the floor, her body has seduced the devil and no human sperm can survive inside its delicious inferno.

My Skin and I

We've been going a long time together; it never gave me any major problems. On the contrary, we've always been good friends and it stuck by me while I felt well inside it. I'm talking about my skin, which seems to be going through a kind of crisis lately. Yes, in the last few days it seems to be cross with me, acting like a betrayed friend.

Why did you do this to me? it seems to be saying. You never set me free any longer. Wool and long sleeves and gloves and socks. This wasn't how we agreed to go through life together. Remember how it was when we got together? You promised me a life under the sun. Not the unbearable kind, but a mild and friendly Mediterranean sun. I thought our life would continue to be like that for ever. We spent most of our time in the open air, walking, sitting in cafés, smiling and taking it easy. I couldn't help getting a bit whiter in the winter, but in the summer I did all I could to make you happy. I'd turn dark, giving you a bronze sheen; I'd open my little pores to give you more happiness when you wanted to freshen up in the dark blue sea. I went along with you and didn't rebel, even when your sea became less clean and heavily polluted. 'What the hell!' you said to me, 'let's forget about what we can't see.' There was an implicit agreement between us: we acted like a happy couple, fitting well together, closing our eyes from time to time, accepting with toleration the natural selfishness of the other. A little allergy here (that I honestly couldn't avoid), a nasty scratching there that you didn't try to repress (when the mosquitoes were high on juicy grapes and sweet figs). But we always made up very quickly and harmony prevailed over and around us.

Look at us today. Poor us! It's been more than three months since you spoke sweetly and softly to me. I know you're cold and miserable because of this permanent winter that we endure in these so-called civilised parts of the world. But whose idea was it to come and live here? You wanted to be free? Look at me: no, just look at you. I've never seen you so miserable. You go out in the garden to bring me immediately back in, covered with blue and red spots. You have a way of getting it all off your chest by screaming at the weather. Lately you've started using learned phrases to explain away your misery: phrases like 'global warming' and 'ozone layer' and other such far-fetched expressions. But what about my frustrations? I tried not to take it out on you, but there are limits to everything, my patience included. What kind of freedom is this you're enjoying, under five layers of clothes? You call this being free?

I see you're feeling hurt! You think I'm being unfair. I admit, you have taken me to some sunny spots around the world lately. But you always bring me back to this grey sky and icy wind. Have you not read the latest medical discoveries? If your skin isn't exposed to sunlight for at least five hours a day you'll suffer from depression! Well, I am your skin, and in the last three months I've hardly seen any light, except for the rays coming from the designer spotlights that you could hardly afford but bought as a miserable consolation.

I see! You want to answer back, but it's obvious that you're no longer convinced yourself. You're starting to doubt your own choices. Your joke about choosing between democracy and good weather is *dépasseé.* The other one about the relationship between the sun and laziness doesn't wash any longer either. Look at all the people around you. They work hard all year long in order to afford a few lazy days in the sun.

Well, why not skip the hard work and return to the sun?

Thus spoke my skin. It sounds reasonable, but I'm too cold and angry to be capable of making the right decision.

Um Kulthum

She stood straight and tilted her head slightly towards her public; I have to bend the aluminium rod harder towards her neck. I stop. I look at her. I have the feeling that she is staring at me. I pull harder and bang heavily on the material but I still can't reduce her to her own figurative self. Here she is again, triumphant in her myth. A winner. A goddess that we can hear, imagine, long for, scream with, cry for. A goddess that can be worshipped but never touched.

'I will make you touchable again,' I say to her while I'm unrolling the black woollen threads that will stand severely combed around her face: an austere, perfect chignon. I stretch the wool but I can't get to her. She is absolutely unreachable. She is definitely looking at me now. She can see me, I swear it. And I, with the millions who worshipped her, cannot see but her aura.

Ah! Ah! she sings, *You keep me waiting, my oppressor, your devastating eyes, if only* ... and millions of Arab women and men sigh listening, late at night, to her complaint, becoming increasingly and desperately addicted to her voice.

No, I cannot carve her mouth. It wouldn't be right, it would be blasphemous. The melodies and the tunes of Um Kulthum, her longing, belong to an ancestral memory, they do not seem to emanate from her lips, her throat or her tongue.

The songs that have marked her fans in their millions will erupt from an abstracted, elliptical and suggested space. Only narrow realism cares about 'truth' in art.

The more I work on her shoulders, the closer I am getting to her secrets. Her shoulders are as stiff as authority! It isn't easy to be a goddess and an entertainer.

Once, on a rare occasion she gave us a little clue. Early this century, she'd left her village for Cairo, 'the mother of the Universe', to witness 'the great disdain in which Egyptian society held all entertainers, and particularly female entertainers'. Not any more, she told herself stubbornly. I want respect and I will obtain it. I can only impose myself if I give them the best of me. And the best of me will always be the best.

I will elongate the iron rod that holds her body. She will appear in her full imposing self. Her glamour will be intimidating. Is it because her father dressed her as a boy in front of village audiences that she never flirted with her fans the way other Egyptian stars did so lovingly? Had she been terrified by the snobbery of cosmopolitan Cairo and defied it by rising beyond anybody's reach, beyond gender limitation?

I'll widen her waist and tighten her lips. I'll pull the iron in opposite directions.

That's it. I'm happy now. I can go away, come back to her later, look at her with 'new eyes' and perfect her image.

I think I understand her better now. She is hiding an oppressive vulnerability behind her carefully composed persona. A cold image of unreachable power. Oh how I wish I can make her reveal her vulnerability. I know it is there, hidden by the stiffness of her posture. I want to see through her. I'll make her big, imposing; I'll hide her behind her dark glasses as she wished, yes, but I'll make her transparent, I'll enable us to see through her persona; I'll make us love her more than worship her.

I look at her and all I see is her severe chignon, her dark glasses and her scarf. My efforts are hopeless. The scarf never left her during her performances. Billie Holiday would never appear on stage without her gardenia. Carving the scarf is relaxing, its drapes have a therapeutic effect on me, and it softens her expression.

But Billie, the other great diva, allowed us to witness her distress. She went to jail, loved with passion and paid dearly for her emotions. Her pain was exposed for all of us to see.

Um Kulthum's pain was revealed in her songs; it was never shown on her face. She never allowed us into her joyous moments; she never had 'fun' with us. Or maybe once, just once, when she asked her lover with a charming flirtatious voice to sing for her. 'Sing for me, sing and I would give my eyes for you.' But can you remember her eyes? They were so often hidden behind her glasses.

I can't fill in her glasses. I'll keep the wire, the plaster and the resin away from their centre. It's because of her begging him to sing that her glasses cannot be terribly impermeable. I'll do it for her. I'll do it out of solidarity.

I am almost there.

But all I've succeeded in doing is to turn her into her own symbol. She is still resisting, long after many women singers imposed themselves and were called 'ladies' in Egypt, long after the lady she became acquired unequalled power, long after she was mourned by millions who cried as if the gods had heartlessly abandoned them when they took her. She is resisting. She can watch me better than I can make her visible.

Truth Smells Bad

I've always had problems with the word 'truth'. Philosophers ponder its meaning, children are taught its merits, everybody swears by it, but somehow it seems to suit preachers best. They, the sermon-givers, bandy it around generously. Truth, I have come to believe, is definitely not the opposite of lying or cheating. For truth is a very controversial term, especially nowadays. Look how keen on truth the prosecutors in the Clinton–Lewinsky case were! There wasn't one detail of this private affair that wasn't eagerly scrutinised in their virtuous aim to reveal the truth. What was done and said – and not done – in bed was disclosed in minute detail in order to establish the truth. What else could lie behind the endless questions concerning the most intimate parts of the president's body, if it weren't for the sake of this holiest of values?

But today this same word causes an allergic reaction for those who cared so much about morality and truthfulness when Clinton's libido was at stake. The same five-letter word that I am tired of repeating. When the lives of thousands of people are at stake, when we want to know why bombs were detonated and hundreds of soldiers sent to risk their lives and suppress others', when the weapons that were so 'genuinely' believed to be the main reason behind this whole mess are still not to be found, the word 'truth' recedes into the background. We're told by the same moralisers that for the sake of good governance we shouldn't know the whole truth. State secrets are supposedly protected to protect us. State secrets are of higher value than the word that took the TV screens of the world into the president's bed.

Truth is starting to smell of bad cigars for me. Not that I'm calling for all of us to become ostriches; this can't be a solution either. But let's get our priorities straight or have the decency to feel a bit embarrassed when we claim to behave in certain ways for the sake of truth. If there's one truth politics and politicians have taught us lately, it's how to lie and defend (their) power in the name of truth. And the more the leaders of the world hide the truth, the more truthful their TV faces strive to look.

It's not only the fault of politicians. The American people were disgusted with the way truth was extracted in the Clinton–Lewinsky case. But there's been a war, and no president or politician has been scrutinised in front of millions of TV viewers. It's as if people believe that nuclear danger and wars are less worthy of the word 'truth' than a couple enjoying themselves in bed.

Let me tell you about another encounter I've had with the word truth. It was very personal and involved no famous personalities, but was nonetheless quite traumatic. A few days ago my friend Joyce invited me to see the premiere of her aunt's play at a major London theatre. To be honest, the play wasn't great. When, at the end of the play, the aunt arrived with a big smile and an anguished inquiring face, Joyce – honest, truthful Joyce – replied, 'It's terrible! I don't like it at all!' The aunt's face was strained, trying to hold back her tears. No, truth isn't always humane.

Lies can be humane, like the lie the young hero of the film *Goodbye*

Lenin kept perpetuating in order not to shock his mother recovering from a coma. She'd been sleeping in an East Berlin hospital all through the period when the Berlin Wall was being destroyed. When she came out of her coma, the doctor told her son that any shock could be fatal. So the young man, adoring his mother, recreated a setting to make his devout communist mother believe that it was the West Berliners who were fleeing the capitalist West, looking for a better life in the communist paradise of the East. Tender and very funny, the film deals with the merits and wrongs of lying in a deeper and more creative way than the leaders of the world today.

For if truth is not always virtuous, lies, I have come to believe, stand somewhere between civilisation and bombing, between the good aroma of a cigar and the stench of a stale and rotten one.

On Anti-Semitism, the Arabs and Evans

Let us for a moment give Harold Evans the benefit of the doubt and grant that his article is a genuine quest for truth and peace. This is, presumably, why he endeavours, over many pages, to expose the evildoings of the Palestinians and other Arabs, and lists the horrible expressions of Arab 'anti-Semitism' that he has uncovered.

Far be it from us to defend or condone the criminal acts committed by the so-called 'martyrs' who, in dying, take with them children, men and women in a bus, restaurant or nightclub. Nor do we wish to deny that there is growing discourse in the Arab and Muslim world that draws from the cesspit of European anti-Semitism. In recent decades, many Arabs have been searching for the reasons behind the total inhumanity of the Israeli occupations. The propaganda of the Israeli state and its Zionist allies deliberately conflates the terms 'Jew' and 'Israeli'. Ironically, it is finally succeeding – in the Arab world. If the friends of Israel consistently confuse opposition to Israel with anti-Semitism, little wonder that some of the victims of Israeli oppression and those who identify with them also end up with the same confusion.

This is where Evans is most astonishing. Like the Zionist establishment, he refuses – despite his protestation to the contrary – to make any distinction between Jewish and Israeli, but he screams with horror when some powerless people don't make this distinction, and he rushes to call them 'anti-Semites', equating them with the powerful Jew haters of the 1930s. Evans is writing for a Western audience; his readers naturally think of anti-Semitism in the traditional European context, in which it was directed against a persecuted minority. In the present Arab context – while still a deplorable phenomenon – it has quite a different meaning.

One could take Evans' analysis more seriously if his prejudices did not lead him to commit ridiculous errors. (Are they just ridiculous? Are they mere errors?) A writer dealing with such an important issue as anti-Semitism who writes: 'the notorious Bolshevik forgery, the Protocols of the Elders of Zion', should have done his homework or at least employed a good editor. This blunder casts serious doubt on his competence to preach on the subject. Even the most virulent anti-communist never dared make such an absurd claim. As is well known to all those who are seriously interested in the subject, the Protocols were a forgery by the Tsarist secret police, directed *inter alia* against socialism, which (along with liberalism) is described as a Jewish conspiracy against Christendom and the old European order. Evans seems to be as ignorant about the origins of the Protocols as the producers of that terrible Egyptian TV soap inspired by the notorious Tsarist forgery. As everywhere in Evans' article, facts are twisted and turned upside-down. He turns one of the main targets of the Protocols into their author – just as his long list of accusations and twisted facts is designed to prove that the victims of today are the Israeli occupiers, not the occupied Palestinians.

If Evans were really seeking a just, peaceful solution for that blood-soaked area in the Middle East he should not only have gotten his facts right, but should also have tried to acknowledge the suffering of the people involved. Evans is (rightly) horrified by the murder of Jewish-Israeli children, but less so, it seems, by that of Palestinian children – which he hardly mentions. And he compels us to play his own game for we must remind him that many more Palestinian children have lost their lives in this conflict. We abhor the need to give numbers and statistics – the idea is somehow demeaning: for every single child who has died in this conflict deserved to have a life and a future and his or her death is a tragedy that destroyed not only their young lives but those of their parents and loved ones.

His bias is made clear from the very first page, where he expresses a hope that '[t]he Israelis may find it in their hearts to forget or forgive the suicide assassins; the Palestinians may find it possible to put behind them the humiliations of occupation'. In this revealing quarter truth, the Israelis are victims of assassination, the Palestinians merely humiliated.

Evans is not unlike those who, in the right-wing backlash atmosphere of the 1990s, kept looking for and citing all the anti-white declarations made by black American activists or poor black youths. The implication was that the most dangerous thing in the US was black racism towards the white American! Those right-wing propagandists – not unlike Evans in the Middle East context today – were able to find plenty of declarations made by Malcolm X, let alone by some new fanatic, equating the white man with the devil. Those were distorted reactions to a long history of inequality, humiliation and lynchings. Malcolm X made many awfully wrong statements in his search for a way out of oppression. But could he be compared to the Ku Klux Klan, or the vicious white supremacists? The whites of the US were not endangered by black nationalist discourse: the relationship of forces was decisively tilted in their favour.

Back to Israel and Palestine and Evans' complaints. There is obviously no mention in his article of the state of the relationship of forces between the Palestinians and the Israeli state. Here are just a few dry statistics, quoted from *Jewish Peace News*:

+ Number of days since the beginning of the current intifada and 30 October 2002: 763
+ On average, number of trees uprooted in the occupied territories, per day: 896
+ On average, number of homes demolished by the Israeli army in the occupied territories, per day: 15
+ Total number of homes demolished: 12,099
+ Area of land confiscated in the West Bank and East Jerusalem by the Israeli authorities since the beginning of the Intifada, in square miles: 63.05 (area of Manhattan, New York, in square miles: 22.7)
+ On average, number of Palestinians injured by Israeli forces and settlers, per day: 27
+ Number of Israelis injured by Palestinians (including soldiers and settlers), per day: 6
+ Number of Palestinian teachers detained by the Israeli army: 75
+ Percentage of Palestinian children, aged six months to five year old, who suffer from chronic malnutrition: 45 percent
+ Number of journalists injured by the Israeli army: 254

These numbers do not include the dead.

Again we are forced in this ugly situation to list tragedies and suffering and to compare them; we are pushed into doing it by the enumeration of wrongdoing by 'the Arabs' to which Evans devotes his article. Wrongdoings they are indeed. But then he writes: 'The brilliance of the whole campaign of anti-Semitism is its stupefying perversity: the Arab and Muslim media and mosque depict Israelis as Nazis ... media and mosque peddle the same Judophobia that paved the way to Auschwitz' (p.14). Please note: not some Arab and Muslim media; not even many Arab and Muslim media; it is *the* Arab and Muslim media that are being accused. Is not Evans deploying against

'Arabs' and 'Muslims' the same stereotypical plot terminology and conspiracy theories that anti-Semites have used against the Jews? Evans has an inflated idea of the Arab media and their organisation. The reality is almost the reverse. There is hardly any organised strategy in the social or political fields; and this is what modern Arab societies suffer mostly from in their development. Evans fails to expose the latest tangible outburst of 'anti-Semitism' in the Arab world, for he does not know this world as much as he claims. *Faris Bila Jawad* (*Horse Without Rider*) is an abominable Egyptian TV serialisation, loosely based on the infamous Protocols of the Elders of Zion. But many Arab intellectuals in mainstream daily newspapers (*al-Hayat*, *as-Safir* and others) as well as Palestinian voices posted through the Internet have condemned it and demanded its suspension. Neither memri (a website) nor Evans seem to be aware of these angry anti-racist Arab voices.

Peace is really in trouble. To secure it, the anti-Jewish upsurge in the Arab world (and for that matter in many underdeveloped countries around the world, seeing a connection between America's misused power and Israeli Sharonist brutality) must be fought. But it does not need voices like that of Evans: they do more harm than good.

Sermons that, echoing Israeli propaganda, condemn Arafat for having aborted the Camp David agreements as a pretext for backing Sharon's destruction of Palestinian society are the work of warmongers, not peace-seekers.

For even if that highly debatable accusation against Arafat were true, how could it possibly justify all the bombing, devastation and killing to which the occupied Palestinians have been subjected? The course of peace negotiations never runs smooth: there are many advances and setbacks. The peace process in Northern Ireland, for example, suffered many outbursts of violence; but did the British then try to bomb all those whom they regarded as threatening the peace process out of existence?

Victims' reactions are rarely purely saintly. The crimes of the victims may often look as ugly as those of their victimisers, but seekers of peace and justice do not use the victim's wrongdoing to whitewash the victimizer.

co-written with Moshe Machover

New Anti-terror Laws are a Red Herring

Why are these people in our country, they are a disgrace, they don't fit in, they want to destroy our European way of life. Islam is a scourge. We have known for hundreds of years that a religion that berates women has no place in our civilized society. Round them up and ship them out.

Alan Emerson, Middlesbrough

They're in our lands, plundering our wealth, killing our women and children, we can't go back, it's time they got a taste of it. They are the real savages and they only understand violence.

Sahib, Birmingham.

These are stirring times in our own backyard. The views above (from IslamicAwakening.com) need to be contextualised and carefully examined, but they are in no uncertain terms a challenge to our Western democratic beliefs, but so too are some of the British government's anti-terrorism proposals. If one holds the belief that the right to free expression is an inalienable one, then the right of some people to say despicable things is the price we must all pay. Tony Blair's plan to criminalise not just direct incitement to terrorism but anything the government may categorise as 'condoning', 'glorifying' or 'justifying' terrorism anywhere in the world is potentially very troubling. We all have problems with preachers spouting hate, and the overwhelming majority of British Muslims are 101 percent behind stringent security measures, and the goodwill to help and trust is palpable, but the new laws could outlaw something far vaguer and harder to define, bundling bookshops and websites into the wrap.

Selectively censoring material deemed to be deviant or dangerous is both foolish and counterproductive. Most of our Middle East customers at Al Saqi bookshop come to us hungry for banned books, for all the books stamped 'censored' back home. We in turn always pride ourselves upon the fact that we are able to bridge that gap, providing a multitude of ideas and visions, from the mystical to the offensive. Censorship elevates the very subject it sees fit to suppress. The Arab proverb 'All that is forbidden, is most desired' springs to mind, and for all those disillusioned young Muslims there will be nothing more potently magnetic than the illicit words of a banned, banished imam. Must we dignify them with such a ban? Are the counter-arguments upon which British society is founded not strong enough?

This climate where a revival of treason laws is rife – with possible charges of common-law offences of treason, solicitation of murder and incitement to withhold information known to be of use to the police – bears, outwardly perhaps, a frightening resemblance to a police state. British Arabs like myself living and working in London, unable to return to so-called 'homelands' with multi-party dictatorships, are tarred with the brush of the Abu Hamzas and Ibn Qatadas. Marginalised, isolated, and on the defensive most of the time, it's little wonder that most of our intellectuals are shunning media attention.

On the literary front, Ziauddin Sardar, Tariq Ali, Tarif Khalidi,

Ahdaf Soueif, Tariq Ramadan, Akbar Ahmad, and others, have written widely and intelligently on many of these issues. *What Everyone Needs to Know About Islam* by John Esposito and *A History of the Islamic World* by F. J. Hill and Nicholas Awde, are great for people wanting to know more about Islam. So is Richard Bulliet's *The Case For Islamo-Christian Civilization*. I have recently rediscovered an old favourite, *Covering Islam* by Edward Said, originally published in 1981, but still amazingly topical. A dear friend of mine always recommends Amin Maalouf and the eloquence of his historical novels; she's currently rereading *Leo the African*. One of Saqi's bestselling books is his brilliant account, *The Crusades Through Arab Eyes*.

An excellent work on *Root Causes of Terrorism: Myths, Reality and Ways Forward* is edited by Tore Bjorgo and a team of international experts and published by Routledge. The book's premise is that addressing the causes of a problem is often more effective than trying to fight its symptoms and effects, analysing the possibilities and limitations of preventing and reducing terrorism by addressing the factors that give rise to it and sustain it. In doing this, a complex tapestry covering a great diversity of groups with different origins and causes appears. But in the final analysis, Bjorgo remarks:

> In counter-terrorism efforts, it is crucial to uphold democratic principles and maintain moral and ethical standards while fighting terrorism. Increased repression and coercion are likely to feed terrorism, rather than reduce it. Extremist ideologies that promote hatred and terrorism should be confronted on ideological grounds by investing more effort into challenging them politically, and not only by use of coercive force.

Which brings us back to our new terror laws: will they prevent further attacks? Do the current powers available to the police and courts not go far enough? How will new legislation affect the normal activities of the average Muslim? Can we ensure that Muslim concerns are taken on board to influence legal decisions? What can British Muslim organisations do to help? Is it not the job of the police and security services to find terrorists and not that of community leaders? What could possibly prevent any future attacks? Do we need to work harder at winning hearts and minds at home, rather than pursue our desire to punish in a game of blame and denial? What are the 'rules of the game'? And to what extent can such rules be applied justly and without misuse?

'The Prophet (PBUH) said, "The highest level of justice is to love for people whatever you love for yourself and hate for them that what you hate for yourself."

In Response

I was ready to be seduced and influenced by Timothy Garton Ash's argument about the objective and subjective elements in the perception of the Madrid terrorist bloodshed and its consequences. That was true until the word 'constituency' caught my attention: 'the terrorists can say to their constituencies in the Arab and Muslim World "mission accomplished".'

These terrorists do not have constituencies. In the Arab world where I come from, they exist as secretly as they do anywhere else. They inform the people through TV channels about their actions and visions. The word 'constituency' is related in my mind to voters (unless it is used here in its very loose meaning of supporters, and those are not defined clearly) and the element of choice through elections is not given its deserved weight by Timothy Garton Ash. The people of Spain have, by marching in millions in the streets and then by expressing their anger through the ballot boxes, taught us all in the West and elsewhere a great lesson. Not only have they shown that the ruled will not accept being lied to by the rulers, but they showed that they are ready to defy the terrorists' threats by marching and occupying the streets of their cities. Their reaction is a whiff of fresh air and hope in the anaesthetised political atmosphere that we are witnessing in our corner of Europe, where many people take it for granted that to be a politician is synonymous with being a liar and that this is often accepted as an unavoidable fact.

Most importantly, let us look at the Spanish reaction from the point of view of an Arab or Muslim person. The coalition, led by the Bush administration, gave many different reasons for justifying their war against Saddam's Iraq. One of these reasons was the benevolent wish to bring 'democracy to this part of the world'. It's not surprising that the majority of people in the Arab world didn't take this reason seriously. I am not going to list the many samples of *deux poids, deux measures*, in particular as far as Israel is concerned (and the Arab–Israeli conflict is still a central political concern for the Arab masses) or as far as the sudden awareness of the dictatorial regimes in this part of the non-Western world is concerned. Exporting democracy as a roughly packaged recipe is already ill-conceived but bringing it to 'the other' after having demonised that 'other' is not the best way to give democracy a good name! Among all the questionable reasons given for the war, democracy was perceived as the least convincing one. Even those who would have hoped for a more democratic society became suspicious if not allergic to the suddenly proposed miraculous cure.

The people of Spain did not want war; their government did not respect their wishes. They suffered, and people in the Middle East and North Africa identified with their suffering like any human being would looking at the horrible pictures of the carnage created by the terrorists' bombs. The people of Spain defied terrorism by marching in their millions to claim their right to their streets, and they showed that choice through parliamentary democracy is really possible. Most importantly, this victorious democratic change is coming from a source that is not perceived as belligerent by the Arab or Muslim populations.

I believe that these lessons are far more substantial than the possible conclusion by some criminals or frustrated people that terrorism pays.

Another important point was raised by Ash concerning Europe and its Muslim and Arab immigrant population. The Arab world and Europe are very interconnected, both historically and because of the growing population of Muslim and Arabs from ex-colonies living in Europe. Today's immigrants are less distanced from their country of origin and less ready to shed all their skin in order to be accepted in 'the West'. This new reality can play a positive as well as a negative role. It is our responsibility (I am speaking as a New European and an Arab) to make sure that defence mechanisms are not standing in the way of an integration that allows the country of origin positive input. The problem of the veil in France has unfortunately been a negative factor on that level. Instead of showing how secularism means more freedom, it has been perceived – not entirely wrongly so – as an attack on 'our customs'. The French Republic has banned the veil in schools, and to compensate made a Muslim holy day a holiday, adding to the many existing Catholic holidays. A more tolerant secular republic would have replaced the holidays given on the occasion of a saint's birth or death or canonisation and allowed people to dress in the manner they wish, while defending those who are punished by their families and the males of the family for getting rid of their scarves.

Art Advertisers

I thought I had seen the worst of this age's obsession with the image and the supremacy of packaging over content until I read the following in *Art-Text*, a very up-to-date and serious art publication:

> Theories of surplus value and dialectical materialism need panache and body language to overcome the leaden feet of history.

I have to admit that in all the attempts at explaining the sudden collapse of the so-called Soviet bloc and the demise of the ideology that had attracted the biggest hearts and very big brains of this century, this one is an innovation. It is a real pearl. So this is the problem! The unexpected development of capitalism, the Stalinist monstrosities, the big changes in the sociology of classes had nothing to do with the failure of Marxism. It was just that the image was wrongly concocted and their advertisers not the best on the market.

I wonder if Marxism had been promoted by some agency like Saatchi and Saatchi, would we all now be earning according to our

Dressing-Readdressing (above and overleaf), with Shaheen Merali. See 'Reading a Book by Its Cover', p. 77.

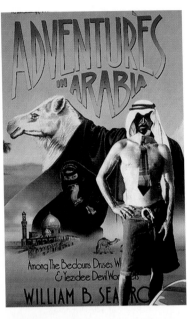

THE FOUR SWANS

THE SIXTH

POLDARK

WINSTON GRAHAM

NEW IN PAPERBACK

Harem Years

The Memoirs of an Egyptian Feminist

Huda Shaarawi

Translated and Introduced by Margot Badran

LE MAROC RACONTE
PAR SES FEMMES

FATIMA MERNISSI

SITER

Women living under muslim laws
النساء في ظل قوانين المسلمين
Femmes sous lois musulmanes

Dossier 19

The many guises of Mai Ghoussoub (above and opposite).

Readdressing the façade of the al-Saqi Bookshop (above). maianna Productions (opposite), with anna sherbany. See 'The Woman in Black', p. 135.

maianna Productions

ORI **ONTAL** as **Lolita**

Writer **Ilana Lucas**
Camera **Vanessa Jones**

LAURENCE OF ARABIA

Ruard Absaroka
as Laurence

maianna Productions

TEXTERMINATORS
Theatrical performance

story telling and dance
with Patricia Kazan
Ane Belen Serrano
Raquel Gribler
and Sandra Socalled

Written and directed by
Mai Ghoussoub

8 March, 2005, 7.30 pm, Lyric Hammersmith
18-19 March 2005 Dominion Theatre Southall

Texterminators was performed in London, Liverpool and Beirut in 2005. See
p. 223.

needs and, perhaps, have an equal share with Bill Gates in Windows! You may think I'm joking, but sometimes I really have doubts, especially when I read magazines like *Art-Text* or when I follow the saga of the 'Sensation' exhibition in the Brooklyn Museum. 'Sensation', as you all well know, is an exhibition of contemporary British art owned by the big collector and successful advertiser Charles Saatchi. Before I remind you of the story, let me make my position clear. Whatever I can conclude, one thing is and will always be sure (I know, I should have learned by now not to trust myself or anybody else declaring 'Never Shall I'): I will stand against censorship, against the mayor and the curators of the Brooklyn Museum, or any other museum, against anybody who wants to suppress artistic expression, however offensive or disagreeable that expression maybe . I am all for taking risks rather than risking the right to freedom of expression. Artistic expression, in particular!

The outcry was against Chris Offili's painting (Offili is the winner of the 1999 Turner Prize) representing the Virgin Mary in which he uses elephant dung collected over three years from London Zoo. This said, I can now indulge in my amusement and amazement at the art and culture that is becoming not only a marketable commodity but a commodity that draws its value mainly from the packaging presented by its authors or promoters, its advertising gurus! Mind you, art has always been a commodity; it just moved from being a commodity enjoyed by aristocrats and the Church to being a commodity more widely available to buyers and collectors, state and national museums included.

Back to Mr Rudy Giuliani and his fight with the Brooklyn Museum, and the private collection of Mr Saatchi. We thought that Mr. Giuliani had lost the battle. The exhibition was more than successful. There were daring people like Hillary Clinton who stood by the museum and the right to freedom of expression, and the losing mayor seemed to have succeeded only in making the exhibition a big news item. The result was long queues of curious visitors, some of whom had never set foot in an art gallery before. But if you've made it in New York politics, you don't give up that easily, your skin is thicker than a first defeat.

Giuliani fights back and launches a new artack. This time he is accusing Christie's and Saatchi of having used the museum (i.e. the taxpayers' money) to promote a private collection, and of increasing its entrance fee. Christie's, having already sponsored the 'Sensation' exhibition in London, had sold some of its works at a price that was now double their pre-exhibition value. After all the fuss caused by the presence of the private collection of Charles Saatchi in very prestigious national museums, the collection was worth much more than its acquisition price. Giuliani is convinced that a prominent advertiser and a private company, however prestigious and respectable, have used a museum funded by the city and its citizens to make more profits and fill their already laden pockets. He considers this matter to be an abuse of power, a trespassing between the private and the public etc ... According to the mayor and his supporters, a shrewd advertiser has shuffled the cards and turned a disgrace into big profit.

I do not know who will win the second round in this fight. All I know is that Saatchi knows better than Marx and Engels how to advertise and promote ideas (most of his artists are, after all, conceptual artists). And the phrase that startled me in the magazine *Art-Text* has lost its absurdity and gained a bitter taste. I can only mention the sad realisation come to in France recently, after the dreadful storm that hit the country: most of the schools built recently have collapsed, while the old buildings still stand firm. The reason is likely to be the predominance of the image and its aesthetics over security. Architects have been more interested recently in the shapes and forms of buildings than in their foundations and solidity.

Now if you think that after all art and advertising both deal with images, you should not be dismayed by the prominence of advertisers on the art scene today. Wait till you see the posters that Benetton is preparing to exhibit all over the streets of Europe. Yes, they are dealing with the very tangible question of the death penalty in the United States. Oliverio Toscani, the photographer who used to photograph supermodels, is now bringing about a new controversy through his images: twenty-six people on death row have agreed to be photographed with 'United Colours of Benetton'. These photos are trying to make us aware of the savagery of the electric chair or the lethal injection. But they're also there to make us buy the products of Toscani's employer, Benetton!

Black Hair, White Beard

Black hair, white beard. Saddam's face appeared on our screens as if it carried two eras in one instant. An old man was still dying his hair black, very black, not long ago. How long does it take for the dye on the hair of a man his age to disintegrate? It seems that not that far back, the dictator was still in control, at least of his own image.

How long does it take for a beard to grow as long and as white as his did? Is this old man, this haggard-looking, hermit-like figure the same man who frightened the hell out of an entire nation for decades and triggered one of the biggest turmoils in world affairs?

When did he stop working on his image, allowing vulnerable white shades to invade his face? A white beard is the privilege of a wise old grandfather, not that of the irascible strong male and fearful fighter that Saddam was eager to promote. Even when he lost power and his statues were felled noisily and dramatically to the ground, Saddam's voice, his perceived appearance, was that of a man with black, very black hair and an even darker moustache.

The moustache is still black, still dyed. It is the beard alone that has fallen prey to the whims of Mother Nature. The white beard of an ageing grandfather is what is so shocking under the expressionless eyes and the same old nose of the new Saddam, Saddam the captive.

Saddam ruled as much through his capacity to create images as through torture and terror. Popular artworks of himself left no space in the imagination of the Iraqi people for anything outside fear and the omnipresence of a powerful, untouchable and almost mythical leader. His black moustache became as familiar as the thick white one Stalin showed his people and the world. Can you imagine Stalin without a moustache? Well! This is why it is so disorienting and unreal to see Saddam, white-haired and dishevelled. That face – with every one of its recognisable features – hasn't changed. You can see this when the camera gets closer, and a still shot appears for a second or two. Nonetheless it's difficult to recognise Saddam, even when you know and you are sure that these features are his and his only.

It is only after I had turned off the TV that I realised that the beard was not what had been the most puzzling element. His beard had triggered a kind of pity for a man for whom I thought I would only ever have hatred. What seemed more unreal and unnerving were the hands (looking for lice?) in his hair, and the dental check-up of this passive resigned man. Was it the broadcaster's intention to assure the public that this is the dictator 'en chair et en os', or are these images conceived to humiliate a man who had worked all his life to create and spread an image of power, control and invincibility?

From Batal (hero) to a fragile old man who seems to be lost and removed, Saddam appeared with the quietness of a sedated person in an old people's home. Viewers, me included, were left feeling silenced and puzzled. Trying to make sense of the clashing images is not easy.

This is why the two men who interrupted Paul Bremer's recent press conference, calling for revenge, looked like badly synchronised pantomime artists, reacting awkwardly and out of context. The action of these two men, screaming their anger and calling for revenge, fitted the image of another Saddam, the Saddam of black hair and black moustache with a clean-shaven face! The elderly-looking Saddam, with his long white troubadour's beard and his eyes looking into emptiness ,brings about a need to reinstall human dignity in this whole sad saga of Iraq's modern history. This is why Saddam should be tried in The Hague, for his rise and fall are on a scale that reaches to the furthest depths of our human condition, the condition of people all over the world.

The Woman in Black

It was many years ago, almost a decade now, when she came to look at *Displaces*, an exhibition about refugees at Shoreditch Town Hall. She was dressed in black. Was she black? Not to me, not to my Mediterranean eye. But in London, the city where we met, she is often referred to as a black artist. Black, a colour that stands by her like the assertion of the French singer Barbara in her song 'Je suis la longue dame brune'. It took me a few years to discover that Anna Sherbany not only dresses always in black, takes photos in black (and white) and claims a black identity, but she has turned the colour into a quest, a conceptual exploration, more: into an artistic pursuit. But anna too was born on the shores of the Mediterranean and her black and white photography is impregnated with the contradictions and grey shades of these shores that have known many exchanges and mixtures and witnessed coexisting truths before black became the opposite of white and white the other side of black.

The gaze of the artist anna and her lens is always subject to the needs of her concept, but it never fails to beat with the heart of anna the woman, the generous observer. There is enthusiasm and plenty of warmth behind the ideas, and in their formulation. You hardly ever see a celebrity, a star or a superhero in her rich portfolio. Her portraits are of friends, neighbours and acquaintances, for it's not charisma or glamour that she's seeking but the 'texture on skin', the depth of the folds and creases accumulated through the years on and in our bodies.

I am looking at her series of portraits exhibited in New York in 1979. *Un-Naked* (Woman Art Gallery 57th/5th) presents men and women placed in exactly the same space, under the same light and photographed amid the same furniture, the framing repeated faithfully. Only (only?!) one element is altered: the subject is photographed once fully dressed and then totally naked. '*Un seul être vous manque et tout est dépeuplé* (One person is missing and the whole world is empty),' said the poet Alphonse of Lamartine. With regard to *Un-Naked*, a piece of cloth is taken off and the whole meaning, the entire visual message is transformed.

anna was still a young art student when – maybe unknowingly or out of pure self-preservation – she raised a question that became fundamental to a generation of artists and cultural analysts a few years later. The question of identity as a social construction through dress codes determined by the gaze of 'the other' and its repercussion is still pertinent and pressing today, more than twenty-five years after anna showed *Un-Naked* in New York.

Visitors to the exhibition were trapped into a room where they couldn't avoid looking at their own reflections while looking at these images. They were bound to 'put themselves in the picture'. The gallery was no longer a container-space, but a forum for dialogue. Here again, I am amazed by anna's discreet and pioneering creation.

There is also the series of portraits, the *Divided Selves*, juxtaposing photographs of women posing twice – once in their ethnic outfits, their 'original' selves, and once in western-style dress. The artist intervention is in the staging: when dressed in their 'original' selves the women look outward from the frame and when their western selves are portrayed, they look directly out at us. Many readings come to mind. Yes, one can speak of the symbolism and power of dress as a maker of identity or as an agent of empowerment, but it is impossible to ignore the effect of nature versus society, spontaneity versus learned behaviour, when faced with these powerful juxtapositions.

I look at anna's portfolio and I pick up another series of readings of the body in space and in colour: a black torso on a white sheet, a white body embracing a black partner both entangled with their own shadows. Entangled physically and metaphorically, in the negative reflection of colour politics.

anna clicks again and again on her camera as if she is reiterating and repositioning her questions. She stages her set, places and replaces her model, moves her flashlight as if she's trying to reformulate the questions that never stop haunting her: her place and ours within the confines of a picture where gender, colour and private-public spaces seem to have been positioned for a unique take.

The juxtapositions of anna sherbany cannot be misunderstood. For me the artist is questioning the colour and colonial hierarchies, the gender dialectics within these parameters. In her work she proceeds as a director in a play in which the theatrical set is a stage conceived to better explore the roles that have been imposed on her/us and presented as objective realities, or as natural-instinctive. The visual pleasure created by the photographs, the dilemmas and ambiguities of the work's final image, speak for the richness of the art for, as with any true art work, there are no blunt messages, there are no clear limits between black and white, between the negatives and their hardly touched positives. The woman in black is the artist of black and white and that of many shades of grey in between.

Maybe I needed to work with anna sherbany to better understand her approach to creativity and her deep involvement in her art: when we embarked on the project *maianna Productions*, an exhibition exploring meaning and identity through the reconstruction and manipulation of the posters advertising the cult movies from the sixties, I realised how much she is first and foremost a photographer, a woman with a camera in her handbag. I observed the perfectionist in her snapshooting and endured her insistence on taking the original photograph again and again instead of resorting to Photoshop.

Our *graduate* was a young black man, not older than Dustin Hoffman, only darker. Our *Lolita* was an Oriental woman sucking on a narguile instead of licking a lollipop. But what pleased anna most was when she discreetly placed a black and white image of the corpse (whose discovery kept Antonioni's film *Blow-up* going) in the background of a poster advertising the film.

Josephine Baker

Today someone called me the Black Venus. I have to admit I sort of like it. And why wouldn't I? I am the talk of the town. Paris is subjugated by my *danse sauvage*. I am the 'wide-eyed woman whose body erupts like a volcano.' My skin is a shelter for the devil, *j'ai le diable au corps*, according to their art critics. The devil hiding inside my skin is responsible for the twitching and the swaying and those untamable spasms of my torso and neck.

I remind them of a giraffe, of a snake, a jaguar and you must have guessed it by now, a kangaroo. Some saw a panther on stage when I appeared. Ha! I came, half-naked, with a belt of fake bananas over my hips, my feet flat on the floor, my knees bent, my stomach tucked in, my buttocks tucked out. This is not ballet, you can bet on it. You have to see their faces. Welcome to Africa, welcome to America, listen to the drums; shudder with my shaking leg; let the steam of violent rhythms take you to a marvellous and magnificent animality.

I am having fun, I need the dance, I need to be loved and admired. I will make them love my contortions and my awkward walk. I will charm them into my earthy source of energy. Come dig deep into the earth for your spirituality, it is not only up there, dig for your multiple souls, cross your eyes with me if you can. Move, laugh and feel how good it is to speak through your body. Enjoy the music and scream, 'Black is beautiful!'

Look! I know there are some people who, proud of their white skin, wrote nasty things about me and my wild dance: 'Her dance makes us revert to the ape in less time than it took us to descend from it.' Yes, this is what they wrote about me, in *Le Figaro* of all places. These people have no sense of humour and are so naïve, to say the least, as to believe that my dance is rich with all these movements, thanks to my so-called spontaneity, my primitivism. They do not know how much training and discipline those movements required. I worked days and nights at polishing the ITCH and MESS AROUND and SHIMMER. I exhausted the mirror perfecting the EYE ROLLING.

Really, white imagination sure is something when it comes to blacks. They think I come from the jungle! I am supposed to be a sample of black energy, of tumultuous primitive instinct, a cry of the maddened flesh.

All this is fine with me. But what I find most hurtful are the words of those who accuse me of playing into the hands of the white man and his fantasies, of looking like a savage in front of those who called us savages!

Would they rather have kept me at the service of Mrs Keiser? She made me scrub the floors and the stairs and the pans and her dirty clothes, from dawn till dusk. I worked and suffered. I was only eight when she punished me for using too much soap for her wash: she shoved my hands in boiling water and I burst so badly that the neighbours took me to hospital.

Honestly, I don't give a damn about those who called my dance indecent or degenerate. I feel proud because I like it when my art is called degenerate. I am in good company. The paintings of Picasso, Nolde and Kandinsky were also labelled degenerate by those who claimed to be more civilised than everybody else.

Calcutta or Kolkata

You know that tune? 'You like potato and I like potahto, you like tomato and I like tomahto. Potato, potahto, tomato, tomahto, let's call the whole thing off.' The great Louis Armstrong made it famous. Today, if he were still alive he'd maybe have added: 'You say "Calcutta"and I say "Kolkata".' The sad lovers here wouldn't have been two black Americans from New Orleans or Harlem, but the British and the Indians. What better example of a love-hate relationship than this ever-intertwined duo. The old colonialist cannot let go of its attachment to this East of his; nor can Britain, as an old forgotten lover; and neither one can forget the embrace and the feuds that are so common in passionate relationships.

A few days ago I witnessed a debate between the head of the Nehru Cultural Centre in London and a very English traditionalist historian who could not stomach the decision of the Bengali government to change the name of this city, which was once the most colonial and cosmopolitan nerve of India.

I wouldn't have given it a second thought if I hadn't fallen in love with a short story written by Amit Chauduri, who was selected recently by the *Guardian* as an author who promises to be one of the great literary figures of the twenty-first century. Chauduri wrote, while studying in Oxford, a low-key homage to his city Calcutta (I use this spelling for I heard that he hates the recent change of name or, to be more precise, of what seems, to a normal ear, to be a change of pronunciation). His story was about a visit he made to his uncle on a Sunday morning; the city was getting ready to burst into life, the sun was friendly. The uncle had settled on the balcony to go through the ritual of having his face shaved by his skilled and talkative barber. The scene felt very familiar to me, and the sounds and smells of Calcutta reaching that balcony reminded me of an uncle of mine being shaved on a Sunday morning on his balcony in Beirut. Chauduri heard about my memories triggered by his story through a common friend, and he liked the coupling of Beirut and Calcutta.

'What if somebody decided to change the name of Beirut? Would you still sing "Tomato, tomahto; Kolkata, Calcutta"?' this friend asked me angrily.

The official from the Nehru Centre answered for me.

'Well, everybody is into identity politics nowadays! We have the right as much as anybody else to define our identity the way we want,' he told the English historian.

'Identity and its obsession is never a one-way thing,' the stiff English traditionalist replied in anger. 'But Calcutta was a little province; it's us, the English, who more than two centuries ago gave it its stature, turned it into the important city it is today. We have given it its name!'

Well, I go back to my encyclopaedia to try to hopelessly find some objective truth in all this mess.

Truth is no longer satisfying, and while the official from the Nehru Centre claimed that the name Kolkata comes from the goddess Kali (the terrible and protective Mother of All), another source, as truthful, claims that before the English, who for obvious colonialist reasons liked to give places they colonised and ruled brand new names, this (then small) town was called Murshidabad.

Calcutta is now going through the same pattern Bombay went through some two years ago: we should be calling it Mumbaye. Some claim that Bombay is the name inherited from its Portuguese origin, Bombaya. In this search for the origin of names and their symbols of identity, one could very easily turn into a schizophrenic historian.

Why is it so important, I kept asking myself while I was watching the angry Englishman in his striped suit? Why is he so worked up? Because when people start relating symbols to identity, they lose their cool. And human beings are never immune to losing their cool. This is how statues started falling in Russia and how most of the statues in the museums of the world stand with broken noses. It would really be more simple and more aesthetic for future archeological sites if we decided to keep the names of places and cities that we have inherited, even if they have been given those names by a dictator or a triumphant occupier. Otherwise all our encyclopaedias would have to have their entries infinitely multiplied.

I agree that my proposal is shallow, but look at St Petersburg: it has changed its name three times this century, and lately the name Leningrad has been reinstituted at certain specific dates and on special occasions (obviously in a democratic effort to please the sensibilities of 'the other's' identity). But what if suddenly more French people start supporting the man who claimed a few weeks ago that the English should not be admitted into the European Community if they insist on keeping the name 'Waterloo' for the station that links the island to the continent. Waterloo is synonymous with French defeat, he said, and it is humiliating for every Frenchman who crosses the Channel and disembarks in a place named after his country's defeat. Now, many French people, let alone other nationalities, do not even know where the original Waterloo stood: not in today's Britain, but in Belgium; but whoever is trying to avenge history through the name of a station wouldn't be bothered with such details.

Symbols and monuments hate details, as does the quest for identity.

Tomatos, tomahtos; Calcutta, Kolkata – maybe the solution is in alternating the appellation. We are, after all, living in five years what our ancestors experienced through centuries of history. I am being serious here. Let us free symbols from an eternal life span. If it is impossible to leave monuments and symbols alone, let us accept their changing fate and the wish of their worshippers to reclaim them or reject them. St Petersburg for five years, and Leningrad for another five. (Atlases are, in any case, becoming redundant in less time than that in most parts of the world.) Freud, who saw the hatred of the other – the stranger – as a form of self-love, a kind of narcissism, would have a lot to write about Calcutta and Kolkata.

Lady Day

Scent of gardenia thrill
Satin, silk, black the colour of pain,
The voice of wounded hearts is raw
Lady! Make it soft, sing me some blues
Reach deep into my sorrows.

Lady sings the blues
Lady has class, Lady has style, Lady has pride
But black is bitter dark in ugly times

Papa didn't have
Mama didn't have
Eleanora was her name
Beautiful bronze little girl
Raped at ten
Jailed for the crime of a dirty old man
You don't need to guess: the judge was white
And the money scarce

Blow your horn sax man
Make it soft and mellow
Let the tune turn whiskey gold and
The voice haunt me crazy.

No matter if the Lady is a queen, a legend, a star
When your skin is black you come through the back door
Front doors are for colourless white faces
Lady cried, she screamed and kicked but the crop remained bitter
Billie pain took up drugs, she drunk an ocean and sung for her man
Men good or bad
Ain't nobody's business if she did
Friends, lots of them, turned shy
'Nobody knows you when you're down and out.'

Bitter crop, black bitter, bitter brown
Forget them, Billie, you're damn too good to care
You're too beautiful for them hate skins to know
Empress, loser, loved and abused
Betrayed and adored
Did you need to suffer so much to become a legend?

Another Asia

I had heard of Tagore. Most of us have. But I had never heard before of Okakura Tenshin. I would never have realised that the author of *The Awakening of the East* was an early echo of the Saidian critique of Orientalism had I not read the impressive book by Rustom Bharucha: *Another Asia: Rabindranath Tagore & Okakura Tenshin*. There are books that disturb your acquired and settled concepts. Bharucha's book on the rise of Asian nationalism, modernity and notions of cosmopolitanism is one of these encounters that unsettle you. Tagore is a figure that we know through his poems, his universality and his scenarios made popular thanks to Indian cinema and the visual beauty of Satyajit Ray. But Tagore developed his views in an era where concepts of identity and nation-building were intermingled and confused to a point that would drive us Middle-Easterners to an even wider sense of confusion.

Okakura Tenshin, who Bharucha considers a pre-Saidian, went as far as calling for Japan to isolate itself totally from the influence of

Western Europeans; he wrote in an ironic tone, in the early part of this century, before the First World War:

> Sanskrit is barbarous if not Germanic, the Taj is a blot if not Italian, Sakuntala is a wonder because Goethe admired it, Vedantism is a treasure because Schopenhauer borrowed from it.

For us in the Middle East the study of Asia, or more precisely Asian identity, or even the concept of Asia could be a study in comparison that would not only help us understand the problem of identity in the post-colonial era, but confirm to us that our problems and intellectual choices are not unique. Tagore and Tenshin, starting with the same quests, end up in total opposition; one opting for universal abstract humanity, the other for obsessive and escapist isolationism.

What is Asia? A geographical entity, an idea, an ethnic term? This question brought as many answers as it did intellectuals who posed it. Those who chose the ethnic response had to hide, for instance, the terrible massacres the Japanese perpetuated on those who were not pure Nippon, and this as far back as the twenties in the last century. One need only read some of Tagore's stories about Hindu-Muslim hatred to realise that the notion of ethnicity in an era of modern state-building is a bomb waiting to detonate. Geography, according to Bharucha, was never settled upon; it expanded and shrank according to people's concepts and ideologies. Asia could mean Japan, India, even include its outmost southeastern limits; it could also mean Iraq.

But more important is the question that seems to be closest to the heart of the author, Bharucha, who is first and mostly a theatre director and an art critic: the *friendship* that was built between these two Asian men – Tagore, who ended up an anti-nationalist, and Tenshin, a symbol of Japan's national pride. Their differences were transcended by their love for art and aesthetics. Their interest in the meaning and deconstruction of the notion of beauty brought them closer than their differing views on the meaning of the Orient and Asia.

They have both become artistic and cultural icons and myths in their 'Asian' countries. India and Japan, so similar, so different. Reading this book, I have learned a lot, not only about Asia, but also about friendship and the power of art to transcend ideas caught in their space and times. Nonetheless, I have not been able to transcend my own sympathies and I still find Tagore closer to my ideals. I wonder if the author, despite all his attempts at being objective, did not help in confirming my sympathy.

Floating Identities

My brother-in-law is a businessman. Last month in Beirut he told me that he'd been in business for thirty years and had had business relations all over the world. You name it: France, Russia, the USA, the Arab Gulf countries and the Netherlands, among others.

'Everywhere, I made business acquaintances. But the Netherlands is the only country where I made friends, real friends among my business colleagues. We are very similar,' he said. Thinking about his remark, I realised that yes, we the Lebanese and the Dutch have many things in common: both our peoples have always looked towards the sea to cross borders and make contact with the world at large; we've both been traders for a very long time, importing merchandise to export it to a third party; and we've always been proud of our tolerant traditions and coexisting religions. The similarities stop there though. We're Mediterranean and have hardly had any industries, hardly any protestant influence on our beliefs and behaviour. We've never had any colonies and we're an even smaller country than the Netherlands. Our citizen is far from being the individual a Dutch citizen is. Nonetheless, my brother-in-law and I still feel at home with the many Dutch people we have met through our professional activities. Speaking for myself, I find this familiarity quite puzzling: after all, I'm French-educated. In school I repeated often: *Nos ancetres les Gaullois*. I know more about French than British history, despite the fact that I lived for only two years in France and more than twenty in the UK. Up to my late teens I knew a lot about Montaigne, Rousseau, Richelieu, Voltaire and I hadn't heard the name Grotius nor, for that matter, read one line of Spinoza. The Netherlands started to figure in my life when, as an adolescent, I read *The Journal of Anne Frank* and later, when in my early twenties, I did the pilgrimage to Amsterdam, the pretty city that promised to offer all that is taboo in my background. Background: I find this word exquisite, so much more revealing and desirable than identity. For identity not only presumes a pure or essential form, but it also comes to the fore in a fanatical way when there is trouble; more often than not announcing it. Background can mean base, a solid one perhaps, but it is also located behind, to be drawn back or sometimes ignored. It's not nagging like a pesky wasp. You can move away from your background; it's a kind of soil in which many realities grow or are planted. Your background is not necessarily your roots; a carrot is a root. We are not carrots. We humans all have some background in one thing or another. The notion of identity is more problematic to me. It is a reflective term; an identity is only defined in contrast to the other. In Europe, the Netherlands included it seems, the question of identity is again on the agenda! Big exclamation mark. For as Eric Hobsbawm, the English/Central European historian, has noted

The word 'identity' did not even figure as an entry in the 1968 *Encyclopedia of Social Studies*, it appeared once and only as psychological identity with reference to Eric Erickson. I would not even dare think how many times the word 'identity' would appear in an encyclopedia on social sciences today.

Yesterday, as a fun exercise, I consulted the Book Bank to see how many books carrying the word 'identity' in the title are in print: there are just under 5,000 in Britain and the US. In 2002 alone, 571 new books carrying the word in their title were published in these two countries. I have to admit that I've used this word myself in the title of my book on male identity in the Middle East, despite my wariness of the entrapments of thinking about identity. (To be honest, I wanted my book to sell, and sticking the word identity into a title seems to be a big boost for sales these days.)

Back to Dutch and Lebanese identity. I read a few weeks ago in *Le Monde* that a survey among the Dutch about identity cards revealed that many were astonished to learn that most of their neighbouring countries had been using them for quite some time. As for my background, I've lived with the idea that an identity card is a necessity; it proves my citizenship or my nationality (two categories that are unfortunately merged into one). And when I lived in France for two years I made sure I carried my ID around at all times, for if I were to be stopped in the Metro or in the street by the police (and, believe me, routine police checks are the norm in Paris) and asked for my ID, I was better off showing something if I didn't want to spend the night in a police station. This use of the word 'identity' as in 'identity card' is a good tool to explore the subject of national identity. A passport for existence as what? A citizen? A son or daughter of Mr and Mrs So-and-so? In my country of origin, the modernisers who've introduced the identity card have included the name of the paternal grandfather and – listen closely – the religious denomination of the citizen carrying it. Here we have three identities rolled into one. This is maybe why I cannot trust the word identity in the singular, and this is why I felt so happy when I became a British national, for I was for the first time aware that I am a person, a citizen who can walk and travel in her city without having to prove her identity. In fact, during the civil war in Lebanon our identity card was a killer. The militias slaughtered many people at checkpoints, who were of the wrong religious persuasion, as revealed on their identity cards. But the article in *Le Monde* I mentioned earlier is very revealing. Dutch society, with which my brother-in-law feels so familiar, and which is so open to the world, can nonetheless seem quite insular at times. Allow me to list the representations of the Dutch that are common: the Dutch are tolerant; the Dutch have the most liberal laws in the world on drugs, sex and euthanasia; the Dutch are self-righteous, down to earth, pioneering, adventurous, self-referential, inventive; their society is multicultural; they are great traders but honest and direct; and last but not least the Dutch are still seen as moving among rows upon rows of tulips under some cute windmill. All these identities/characteristics are quite heterogeneous. They carry, like all clichés, some truth. But in our very rapidly changing context, how deep are these truths? How much can they still define a society that is inside a changing Europe, a globalised world and an era of immigration, not towards the colonies but from the ex-colonies themselves?

Isaiah Berlin gave British society as an example of good multiculturalism, insisting that for the society to keep its positive characteristics and still be peaceful there should be one dominant core that has its culture and values at the centre of society, and other (I guess immigrant) groups and cultures within that country can have their own identity as long as they recognise the primacy of the dominant culture. This seems fair enough at first sight. But this assessment is based on a vision of a stagnant 'core'. As if white English culture, for example, was unified, with no inner contradictions or competing factors. It's also based on the belief that this core culture is hermetic to surrounding influences. It assumes that identity is not in constant flux and its basic traditions not being constantly reinvented. Nostalgia is one of the best feeders of fiction. It is essential. But it does not and it is not asked to construct the present.

The Dutch can bring to the world many positive elements and societal examples. And they have been doing that on a cultural level. I have happily witnessed this with the Prince Claus Fund. The cultural attitude of many Dutch organisations is the best homage to Hella Haasse's complaint in 'Forever a Stranger' (or 'Oeroeg') when she wrote: '... And Oeroeg ... It is superfluous to admit that I did not understand him, I knew him as I knew Telaga Hideung – as the sparkling surface of a crater lake – but I never fathomed the depths. Is it too late?'[1] I may sound very unconnected and scattered. But through these patchy elements and examples, I am trying to relate Europe and the Middle East as I see them today. We have a long, not always happy common history. Once we thought of Europeans as 'Barbarians' and we went on unaware that Europe was developing while we were lagging behind. I'll quote this very lucid passage from Amin Maalouf's *The Crusades Through Arab Eyes* (having defeated the Crusaders, whose civilisations were considered to be backward and barbaric):

> The Arabs refused to open their own society to ideas from the West. And this in all likelihood was the most disastrous effect of the aggression of which they were the victims ... And in fact the Franj (Western people) learned Arabic, whereas the inhabitants of the country, with the exception of some Christians, remained impervious to the languages of the Occidentals.

Morale de l'histoire, as La Fontaine would have put it: never believe that you always know better, or that the others have nothing to teach you. But back to the Dutch and my Lebanese background. Even three times smaller than the Netherlands, our identity is manifold and complex: Arab? Mediterranean? Some say Phoenician; half-westernised; Muslims? Yes, even in the country where we cannot move without an identity card, each has many identities. Like anywhere else in the world today; hardly any island remains totally

---

1.   *Forever a Stranger and Other Stories*, Oxford in Asia Paperbacks, 1996

isolated. When, incapable of sustaining our democratic institutions and tolerant coexistence in a changing regional environment, we decided to defend one sort of regressive identity (our confessional one in this case) we collapsed into chaos, civil war and barbarity. The Dutch do not face such risks, not only because they and their regional environment have built some immunity after the horrors of the Second World War, but because, as Adriaan van der Staay has written, 'The Netherlands appear to be a culturally facilitating country without an identity, and this in turn may seem to be their most characteristic identity'. I guess Adriaan means without defensive insular, identities. I hope this quality will mean the Dutch will keep on changing within a changing Europe and a changing world, giving us and the arts more with more fusion and creativity, and why not lots of colourful tulips as well?

Monopoly

I do not know anybody who hasn't at one time in his or her life speculated in property. I mean speculated on this colourful square board called the Monopoly game.

This is how, as a kid growing up in Beirut (the game is for the over eights!), I was fully aware, along with many other kids, that Mayfair is much more posh and thus more expensive than Soho. Avenue Foch, or Rue de la Paix for the French-educated who invested in the French Monopoly, was obviously a place to invest in if one could afford it, while the area of Les Halles was to be avoided at all costs. It was only later in life, after having outgrown Monopoly, that I realised – visiting the areas that I'd bought, won and lost – that this colourful board game may have been right on the money with regard to property speculation but it was totally wrong as far as my idea of desirable urban living was concerned. Yes, I definitely prefer Bloomsbury and Shoreditch to Mayfair, and I wouldn't want to spend one minute in Avenue Foch if I could have a flat in St Germain des Pres.

Today I'm revisiting the most famous game in the world, not as a person interested in property, not as an investor or an economist, but as a person who is fascinated by the universality of this game that is played in over eighty countries worldwide, and that knows no setbacks. Today is Monopoly's seventieth birthday.

I've never given this classic board game as a gift to a child. I never felt at ease with games that were concerned with getting children to enjoy accumulating riches. But it seems that my not buying the Monopoly game has had zero effect on its ongoing commercial success. Its promoters are proud to advertise it in the following terms:

> An estimated 500 million players around the globe have enjoyed the game since its creation in 1935 ... The Monopoly game has to be the biggest builder in America! Who else manufactures a million houses in a year?

Not my idea of good or positive. Nonetheless, business people, professionals and artists alike (I mean real artists) admit to having had a lot of fun playing Monopoly. Rare are those who shriek at the concept behind the title (to monopolise!!!) of the game itself. Even Jane, my most politically correct, anti-globalisation, Buddhist, egalitarian friend, didn't think twice before buying if for her son's tenth birthday. When I joked with her, saying, 'So now you're not banning the word "monopoly" in your home, while you're ready to travel to Porto Allegre to scream against it?' she answered, 'You obviously don't know the story of this game. If you were better informed you'd know that this game is originally a socialist game!'

Trust Jane to have read at least two books before selecting the right game for her son! Well, guess what?

> The original purpose of the Monopoly game was to teach the evils of exploitation (it was entitled the Anti-Monopoly) and was conceived by socialists rather than its alleged inventor and the

giant game maker Parker Brothers who has no right to monopolize it (m not capital here).

Yes, Jane had read the book by Ralph Anspach, *The Billion Dollar Monopoly Swindle*, which tries to prove that the alleged inventor of Monopoly, Charles B. Darrow, who, according to the story, had invented the game during the Great American Depression when he was unemployed, is no more than a copycat.

So the story of the Monopoly game owes its phenomenal success to the same values that are at stake in the game itself! Speculate, and come out on top by bankrupting another speculator ... Thanks to Jane's erudition I can at least console myself in the belief that if I enjoyed playing this game with my schoolmates during the holidays it was because I knew unconsciously that the game was originally an anti-Monopoly one!

But here I am again, thinking of psychological motivations, while the executives of the Monopoly company are busy re-evaluating the real estate value of the areas drawn on the boards. Yes, Soho is no longer that cheap, and Les Halles is most probably unaffordable. And guess what? The new board is getting rid of train stations. They're part of the past. They're being replaced by airports. There's no room for nostalgia. You can only dream about buying a hotel near a noisy airport and making the biggest profit imaginable.

Countryside Lovers

'Where are you going for the New Year's break?' This question is all you hear in London throughout the month of December. Millions are leaving London for the quiet and green (ever-green) countryside. Obviously, you must be leaving town and getting closer to Mother Nature as well.

Not me, you can bet on that! Not only do I like cities, but I like them even more when all those who seek the purity of the air and the freshly damp earth are getting out. The city between Christmas and New Year is great. Most importantly it is free from all those who dream of leaving it, turning it into pure delight for those who appreciate it. When can you find tickets for a play that has been fully booked, months in advance, if not when all those who are breathing fresh air and digesting their turkey, looking blissfully at the sheep through their windows, have deserted the theatres? Moreover, less famous artists and young, less established performers can find a slot to show their work in this period; and believe me their experimental and creative output brings a breeze of fresh air far more invigorating than all the unpolluted drifts circulating in the countryside.

When can you find parking spaces the moment you decide to park, in the centre of town – yes, in the very centre of town! – after all the car owners have decided to fill their vehicles with gifts, puddings, nuts and warm clothes and to drive away from this same centre? When can you book a tennis court with another city rat without having to wait half an hour on the club's busy lines except when people are struggling with their choice of chocolate instead of sweating over a ball? And if you don't play tennis, you have the gym, this urban invention par excellence. The gym is almost empty during the festivities, except for you and some people who have no aunts in the countryside to visit. As it happens, Londoners with no aunts in the countryside are mostly Asian, African or Latino. This means that the music you listen to while doing your stretches is far superior to the usual repetitive electrical rhythms that the majority imposes on the minority among the cardiovascular-conscious. Let's be honest, at the risk of being politically incorrect: it's much more enjoyable to push thirty kilograms back and forth with Bob Marley's voice than it is to bring the same kilos in and out, pumping your lungs over a synthesiser that despises human musical artistry.

And what about food and culinary pleasures during Christmas and New Year? I bet the city is less carnivorous than the countryside. Don't ask me why, I couldn't tell. But it seems that those who like wildlife and the sight of cows, also like to eat more of those cows and put more lambs in the oven. I have to admit that I have no statistics to prove my point. It's just a feeling. You could accuse me of being prejudiced and unfair but I think that I'm not a great milk drinker and I don't adore meat either precisely because I love the city. So I could do with fewer animals around and more cinemas, concerts, theatres and coffee shops. All of these don't feature prominently in the rural ethos, while they offer themselves to you with plenty of seats in the city during this period.

Mind you, lovers of the countryside or not, these millions of urban defectors suddenly rush back to invade our spacious city in order not to miss the sales.

'They want to have it both ways,' I tell the lady driving the car parallel to mine and stuck in a traffic jam near a shopping mall. 'They could have stayed living a simple life, at one with nature, leaving this consumer evil space to us!'

'All I can hope', she replies, 'is that next year they'll suffer more on the road back and get stuck on over-busy motorways for a few hours more.'

I don't feel revengeful like she does, but there is definitely some fairness in her statement.

The Balcony

Two little girls slowly sip their freshly squeezed orange juice on the balcony overlooking the courtyard one floor below. The boys downstairs are playing noisily, vigorously kicking and fighting over a ball. Sure enough, the ball bounces higher than desired and lands in Sitt Nazik's garden, just in the midst of her beloved gardenias. It takes no time for the widow to come out screaming, looking as desolate and as broken as the poor gardenias.

'You impolite, cruel boys!' she hurls, pointing her thin finger at the five or six bewildered faces. The young boys shrug their shoulders; poorly suppressed laughter narrowing their lips. Are they ashamed or defiant? The little girl cannot really tell.

'They are not bad boys; they are from our building. They are the sons of Sitt Josephine and Madame Nadia,' she tells her older sister, who has taken Sitt Nazik's side against the naughty boys.

The little girl envied the children of Sitt Josephine: twelve boys and girls spilling endlessly outside the limits of their doorstep. Every day at dusk, on her way home from school, the little girl wishes she could stay in the courtyard and join the boys and play football with them.

Sometimes the boys sit on the three steps that lead into her building's courtyard, discussing the game with nonchalant but expert gestures. These three steps are the sacred line that separates the outside – the others – from her own world, that of her protective father, her sweet mother, her older sister and their loving old maid. Many times, crouched on her knees, her head stuck to the balcony's railings, fitted inside their carved arabesques, she had looked enviously at the 'grown-ups' who transgressed freely the decisive steps.

Now that she wakes up in her pretty room, now that she is no longer as little as before, living on the fifth floor of a modern building, she wishes that she could sneak out onto that large old balcony again for a few minutes, as she and her sister used to do before leaving for school. During those precious minutes the two little girls would marvel at the sight of women in pink and blue *robes de chambre*, hurrying out of the buildings beyond their courtyard, arguing unashamedly with the ambulant vendors over the price of courgettes, oranges and other colourful merchandise offered on their carts. How she misses the chants of the fruit sellers, their tunes overlapping in a wonderful cacophony. Only the song of the Mazout man (fuel man) seemed sad and plaintive. *Mazout, mazout*, cried his ancestral voice. The little girls never saw the Mazout man; they only heard his sad song, for he always travelled before the city had awoken. Now, in their modern flat, in the new building, when she and her sister leave for school in the morning, they go through the garage door, from the back of everything; never meeting other children on their way out, never hearing any voices escaping through the doors and the windows of the homes looking into the courtyard. Now in this 'much more comfortable home' she has no taste for the mornings, for she has lost the view from the balcony and the chants of the street vendors.

When they lived in the old house, looking over the courtyard from the tiled balcony, the little girls lived in a world that extended far beyond their small family. As soon as they walked on its oriental tiles, beyond the tall arched windows, other lives, different mothers and fathers came into their world. The little girls had a first encounter with the violence that took place 'outside', on the bad streets of the city.

The little girls have no reason to worry about the 'bad streets', for they existed somewhere far beyond the three steps at the other end of the courtyard: Sami, the son of Sitt Nazik, comes running into the courtyard, looking dishevelled and terrified.

'The poor woman is alone, and she cannot control her wild adolescent boy,' the little girl hears her mother say with a sad voice. 'He plays pool for money and is mixing with bad boys.'

The little girls are slowly eating their biscuits, watching the courtyard through the carved railings. They are terrified: the bad boy follows Sami into Sitt Nazik's garden. Sami is covering his face with his arms to avoid the hard blows of the nasty big boy. They hear Sitt Nazik pleading and crying. The little girls are called in and moved away from the balcony. But what they have just seen will never fade away; they have lost their pampered vision of a world made only of nice people and happy stories. The balcony reveals a deeper and more complicated view on things and so will they.

Here, inside this modern and efficient architecture, in this tall building with its grey lift and silent neighbours, only novels and the TV screen tell you about the others and their worlds.

The little girl is less little and she remembers her mother picking fruit from the tree that grew into the tiled balcony. Glamorous and elegant, her mother smiles, extending her arm towards the fruit while she releases her long black hair away from her beautiful face. Was there really a fruit tree on that balcony or has she seen it in an old photograph in her parents' red velvet album? Photographs, after all, often shape reality; they are our memory's alibi. Memory and history, I heard a critic say the other day, speaking about Proust and his *A la recherche du temps perdu*, are shaped by the novels we have read and the stories we were told more than by real facts. The balcony of her old house is the little girl's childhood, it is her dreams and fears.

The little girls are giggling and laughing: big buckets of water are poured over the tiles and the maid is telling them to refrain from stepping in the water with their bare feet. Their laughter is as clear as water, their happiness as simple as the geometric design of the tiles and their matt brown colour.

The balcony of their old house is full of memories; the narrow balcony of their new flat, looking directly, from very high up, onto the city, has no tales to invent and no stories to tell.

Contradictions

This is the country of contradictions. I have heard this phrase about Lebanon a thousand times! Sometimes it is said with admiration, sometimes with disdain, often with irritation; but whatever the tone, the response is always definitely acquiescent. No wonder I have a tendency to dismiss such declarations about Lebanon as 'the country of contradictions' as boring clichés. After all, where in today's world is not full of contradictions?

So until last week, I was still very dismissive of all those who think that our country of Lebanon is special in the domain of opposites and differences. What happened last week is that I went to see the women's demonstration for al-Haqiqa that filled the streets of downtown Beirut. Since the death of Rafiq Hariri, women have become very outspoken politically in Lebanon. They've organised many events, sit-ins, demonstrations, and they argue more passionately if not more loudly than their male compatriots.

A nice long cortége, a beautiful enthusiastic white cortége (the organisers had asked women to wear white scarves on their shoulders), moves from the Place des Martyrs towards the scene of the crime. The women's demonstration is impressive in its size but also in its variety; feminists walk alongside members of women's charities, housewives and professional ladies, all on the street to express their anger at this abject violence.

Suddenly, after the now-familiar slogans calling for unity, freedom and truth, a large group of women comes marching along, chanting enthusiastically: *Ya Lahud Nzeil Nzeil, Hal Maq'ad Baddu Rijeil.*

I couldn't believe my ears! Did I hear *Rijeil* as in manly, as in *gada*, strong, tough? Did I hear *Rijeil*, meaning not a woman? There are women among this group who are consciously investing a public space and calling for machismo to lead the country and to lead them! These women come dressed in white like all the other women who have joined the demonstration; they have joined a peaceful march, full of colour and vibrant with life and efficiency, to call for a person wearing a dark grey suit to lead them? A few women from another section of the group try to override the slogan with ... *Bado Niswain* instead of *Rijeil*, but to no avail; the group that wants a *Rijeil* is not listening.

Now I have to admit that as far as the rhyme is concerned, *Nzeil* and *Rijeil* are more in harmony than *Nzeil* and *Niswain*. But ordinarily aesthetics would be sacrificed for the sake of common sense. Not in Lebanon, where aesthetics rule and the obsession with the way things are presented is as important as the things themselves. Take, for example, these slogans printed in large format on billboards along the motorway leading from Beirut to Tripoli: YES TO INDIVIDUALITY, YES TO TOLERANCE. You might be forgiven for thinking that these are the slogans of a new liberal party, or that they're advertising the philosophy of John Locke, or a book by Isaiah Berlin. But you'd be wrong! These slogans are for the latest stock of designer jeans and T-shirts Aishti is promoting.

Individuality is represented by the different colours, but, as far as tolerance is concerned, your guess is as good as mine. Big ideas are good for fashion, and fashion and design are as big as ideas in Lebanon.

I have to admit that I sympathise with the capacity for turning serious matters into fun as much as I loathe the obsession with empty form. Still, if I had no choice but to select one thing or the other, I would definitely choose superficial tolerance over substantial uniformity.

Chewing Gum, Insatiable Women
and Foreign Enemies

'No blood spilled and no battles. Here is the chewing gum that unleashes sexual instincts with stimulating effects that exceed the power of 30 doses of a medical sexual enhancer.'

This is the latest weapon used by the Israelis against the 'Arab body', claimed the liberal Egyptian paper *al-Ahrar* in June 1996.

The story of the 'Israeli Chewing Gum' presents the fearful spectre of a gum that unleashes sexual desires while at the same time rendering its consumers sterile. Who was the first to come with this stunning revelation? *Al-Ahrar* or some unknown source no doubt claiming to have access to the most reliable authorities on the matter? The newspaper assures us that Israeli research in the field

has shown that the sexual excitement brought about by the chewing gum is not an end in itself. The ultimate object is the negative consequences of this stimulation, for if this gum increases the activity of the sexual glands in an extraordinary way, multiplying it by at least 50 times its normal rate, the chewing of this gum, even if only rarely, causes impotence through the destruction of the reproductive organs in the metabolism. The whole thing will result in a total ceasing of sexual activity among the inhabitants of the Arab countries within a few months .... And the aim lying behind this infamous Israeli plot is the decrease of the birth rate in the Arab countries in order to narrow the broad demographic gap between the Arabs and Israel.

Such a dramatic revelation could not be ignored by the rest of the media! The daily *al-Arabi* (an Egyptian Arab nationalist paper) proudly declared that it had exposed the chewing gum plot before anyone else: 'the MP [Member of Egyptian parliament] Fathi Mansour, relied on our information in order to carry this disaster from a mere newspaper campaign to an actual item on the agenda of the People's Congress.'

We know all too well that the dividing line between rumour and information can be blurred and that it may even disappear entirely. What is significant to me in the case of this magical chewing gum is not to assess how trustworthy the sources of the mentioned journals are, nor if the editors of these sensational articles seized an irresistible rumour and carried it with the authority of the written word, nor, conversely, to discover whether this 'reliable information' draws the strength of conviction from the public opinion that it merely seeks to confirm. What is fascinating is the power of this *innocent-looking* chewing gum on the imagination of the readers of the newspapers mentioned above, as well as on at least one active member of the parliament. I am describing this chewing gum as innocent-looking for I saw its picture printed in one of the Egyptian papers during those troubled days: printed in black and white, on thin grey paper, this chewing gum could indeed 'be very easily mistaken' for the little white squares produced by the Chicklets company or the Lebanese Ghandour factory as the newspapers warned us. I am also speaking of the authority of the written word because even the serious *al-Nahar* newspaper in Lebanon reported the story of this enchanted and poisonous gum in the most serious terms, relating the facts in a news dispatch without comments and with no mention of the word rumour, or claim or allegation. 'A brand of Chewing gum and drops from Israel behind the uncontrollable sexual excitement of Egyptian girls' is the title of the dispatch from Cairo reported by *al-Nahar* on 9 June 1996. The news dispatch reveals that according to *al-Akhbar* newspaper in Egypt the MP Fathi Mansour has declared that 'the story had started in one of the regions' Universities, where many cases of rape were reported. There were up to 15 cases of rape. What is new is that the girls were the violators in some cases and they perpetrated the rapes because of their untamed sexual desires.' He added that he investigated this chewing gum and discovered that it was smuggled in through the Israeli-Egyptian borders.

If rumours draw their strength from the perception of people who believe them, repeat them and spread them, we ought to take this fantasmic chewing gum seriously and try to understand why the need to believe in its existence is stronger than the need to question the credibility of the whole story. After all, a real parliamentary committee was designated by the People's Congress of Egypt to study the matter and arrest the culprits. *Al-Ahrar* declared in the same famous article of 25 June 1996 that this chewing gum had been invented by a Mossad agent working with the K G B and that Yitzak Rabin himself had given the order to increase its production.

I would like to investigate the driving quest behind these rumours. What do they tell us about male fears and sense of identity? Are they signs of threatened masculinity or a symptom of the renegotiation of gender relations and sexual attitudes in Egypt and in the Middle East today?

Why chewing gum? Could it be because women are its main consumers and that the fear of the chewing gum effect is actually a fear of women? This chewing gum is going to trigger a large sexual appetite among the female population. And what choice are husbands left with? They may quite understandably be tempted to use this miraculous enhancer to satisfy their insatiable wives, but the price paid for this short-lived super-virility is enormous: eternal impotence, the end of their progeny, and endless shame. How could a father or a brother preserve his honour if his daughter or his sister have an uncontrollable sexual drive? All the masculine fears are exposed and challenged by these little white squares. Many male fantasies may also be triggered by these female rapists. These tiny white squares act with the swiftness and the efficiency of an invisible spy; they are here to threaten a virility that has lost its guidelines. Only the devil, dressed as a superpower, hiding within these tiny squares can be so astute in his quest to emasculate the ordinary citizen.

Who said that it was easy to be a man?

Lately, the Arab publishing world has been prolific in 'educating' the modern reader with texts retrieved from a past that was less inhibited by an austere approach to sexuality and its pleasures. In the last ten years the writings of Sheikh Nefzawi, Ahmed Bin Selman, al-Siyouti and many others have been published in at least ten new editions each. These manuals – written in good faith a few hundred years ago for a good cause and to better serve the believers in the prophet – have often been often seized by the agents of censorship in the modern and national Arab states. This seizure has in fact had the effect of increasing their popularity and their readership, generating endless reprints of popular as well as luxurious editions. Even if a few women do purchase these manuals, their readership remains above all male and if you visit Arabic bookshops, you will see that they are piling next to Fukuyama's *End of History* or Paul Kennedy's *The Rise and Fall of the Great Powers* without either their readers or the booksellers, feeling them the least bit anachronistic or out of place.

You may be asking yourselves what is the link between the Israeli Sexual Chewing Gum and Sheikh Nefzawi's *al Rawd al 'Ater* (The

Perfumed Garden), written and published at the beginning of the fifteenth century, or Ahmed Bin Selman's *Ruju'u al Sheikh ila Sibah* (The Rejuvenation of the Old Man), first published in the sixteenth century) or al Tijani's *Nazhat al Aruss* (The Bride's Promenade), or al-Siyouti's *Kitab al-'Idah fi 'Ilm al Nikah* (The Book of Explanations in the Art of Fornication) or ...? The list is becoming very long indeed. How could these texts written for the glory of Muslims have anything to do with this plot 'aiming at destroying them'? Could these popular manuals, written before Christian austerity invaded the scene, have something to do with the fantasies and the fears expressed by those who spread the chewing gum rumours or those who were pretty eager to believe them?[1]

Many centuries have passed since Sheikh Nefzawi wrote his sexual manual. No modern Arab man, writing about sexuality and its pleasures, would dream of thanking God for having created women's vagina for men's pleasure and having created men's penis for the pleasure of women (for it is with these sentiments that the Sheikh's famous book opens). Indeed, when a publisher decided to reprint the book in the 1990s in Beirut, the 'morality police' had it banned and the edition was – in principle – confiscated. The result as you may very well have guessed was the appearance on the market of a multitude of other editions. Where Sheikh Nefzawi felt he was accomplishing a religious and civil duty by writing his manual (dedicated originally to a vizier of Tunis), the modern religious authorities want it banned as pure pornography.

I have still to explain the reason why I am referring to these blessed sexual manuals, when I have started by mentioning the story of the famous (infamous) Sexual Chewing Gum. I believe that the relation lies in the fears and fantasies of men who may have changed

---

1. I do believe that Christian sexual morality has deeply impregnated the modern Muslim world, and that many fundamentalists' rejections of Western depravity are merely and unconsciously reconstructing Western–Victorian pre-sexual revolution attitudes towards sexuality. Among today's secular elite, this attitude is expressed in terms of high culture versus vulgarity.

drastically in the last century, as far as their morality, social norms and existence are concerned, but whose views on sexual performance and women's desires are still deeply imprinted on their inherited memory and have not adjusted accordingly. The relation is in men's tortured relationship with their own 'masculinity', with its meanings, demands and projections. The status of women, despite all the recent backlashes in Arab-Islamic societies, has changed dramatically; their impact and their presence in the socio-economic sphere has drastically increased, their images on the pages of popular magazines and on TV screens are limitless in their variety. This is true in even the most misogynistic corners of the Arab world: how can men not have changed accordingly, be it in one direction or the other? The most revealing expression of this dichotomy is the early reprinted edition of Sheikh Nefzawi's *Perfumed Garden* by a Lebanese publisher in the late sixties. The entrepreneurial spirit of this publisher cost him a few nights in prison, the authorities being totally oblivious to the irony of the extremely kitschy and vulgar cover to the edition. The 'artist' who had conceived the cover had obviously cut, very roughly, an image from a fifties American fashion magazine, in which a very slim, high -heeled and elegantly dressed lady, whose face is hidden under a wide sophisticated round hat, appeared holding a tray. But instead of the drinks that the original model carried on the tray, the publisher had stuck on Sheikh Nefzawi's cover a large penis for the lady to carry! The saying 'old concepts in modern dress' had never been more to the point.

Nefzawi asserts in his perfumed garden that 'women are never sated nor tired of copulating ... Their thirst for intercourse is never quenched'.[1] And Bin Selman writes in *The Rejuvenation of the Old Man*, confirming his predecessor's vision of female sexuality: 'Some have affirmed that women's sexual appetite is many times superior to that of men ... The weakest sexual desire among women is more

---

1.   *al-Jins Inda al-Arab*. al-Jamal publishers, Koln 1997 vol. 1, p. 91

powerful than the strongest male desire.'[1] These statements are told in the best tradition of storytelling: we are entertained with the stories of slaves or princesses who have made love to hundreds of males without ever tiring and who ask for more and better sex.

If we take the statements of these pious men as objective and indisputable facts (and this is how they conceived and presented them originally), we can be sure that it must have seemed impossible for a man to satisfy a woman and to match her sexual demands. The task must have been terrifying for she 'is never tired of copulating' and 'her sexual appetite exceeds his'.

What a frightening perspective for our males if they happen to give credence to these authoritative manuals. If women have such an insatiable appetite – and this assertion is stated as a scientific reality by many of these learned men who speak with authority of the Fiqh (Islamic law) and with their apparently great knowledge of biology – why would they not seek fulfilment in other, and more, men? The fear is real: it is the fear of not being up to matching the masculine ideal, of failing to perform like the stud women are supposed to want, to desire and indeed to desperately need!

If the seclusion of women was the answer that came easily and logically to many anguished males in the past,[2] what are they to do when the barriers between the sexes are relaxed, and these very sexuated beings – their women – are working in mixed environments? When they walk freely on the streets and share the overcrowded public transport of overpopulated cities?

It is becoming more difficult to be a male!

Listen to Nefzawi quoting the poet Abu Nuwas: when sexually aroused 'women fail to distinguish the master from his slave'.[3] According to Bin Selman in *The Rejuvenation of the Old Man*, al -Alfiya ('the

---

1.   Ibid. vol. 2, p. 151

2.   Mernissi, Fatima. *Beyond the Veil*. Saqi, 1985

3.   *al-Jins Inda al-Arab*, Vol 1, p 92

thousander'), who owed her name to the thousand men she had had sex with, had acquired a great experience in keeping a man erect for days on end. She held a salon where women gathered to seek her advice and collect recipes for that purpose. It seems that honey, onions and the camel's milk are the essential ingredients against the undesired lapses in men's virility. How far are these ingredients from those needed to produce these treacherous small white chewing gum squares!

Reading through these volumes of sexual treatise, one is struck by how familiar and widespread these male fears and fantasies are in all societies! Very often, our authors confuse their own fantasies and dreams with their objective and scientific conclusions. And this is quite natural and human. The length of a male penis is one of these obsessions that all these learned men take for granted as far as the satisfaction of their demanding and permanently aroused women are concerned. Remember, these books that deal at length with the needs and desires of women are written by men: when the poetess Leila al-Akhiliya is asked about the desired length of a man's penis, she answers that ideal is when it reaches twelve inches; and when the penis of a man is less than six inches long he has to compensate with other qualities and through other means.[1]

To make men's life more difficult, our manuals believe in the limitless capacity of women to concoct stories, to resort to the most ingenious ruses in order to reach their aim. Men are less shrewd and over-sexuated women with powerful brains will always triumph! 'The wiles of women are innumerable, they can mount an elephant on the back of an ant.'[2]

The writer I like most among our sexologues by far is Shehab Eddin al-Tifashi (born 1184): he introduces his book *Nazhat al-Albab Fi Ma La Yujad Fi Kitab* (The Mind's Promenade Inside What No Book Will Tell You)[3] by thanking God for blessing men with the

---

1.   Ibid, Vol. 1, p. 40
2.   Ibid, Vol. 1, p. 99
3.   *Shihab al Din Ahamad*, al-Tifashi, *Nazhat al-Albab Fi Ma La Yujad Fi Kitab*. Riad el-Rayess Books Ltd, London 1992

capacity to have fun and to enjoy lightness. Al-Tifashi is the least misogynistic among his colleagues. He mixes many literary genres in his book, telling jokes, quoting poetry and referring to science and logic in order to tell us about women, their desires, their sexual tastes and their ruses. He states the elements that constitute and produce the perfect adulterer. According to our proficient author, to be a perfect adulterer a man needs:

- To be young for women prefer them younger
- To wear perfume. Women's desire is aroused by nicely scented bodies
- To bath frequently and colour his hair with henna. Henna should be used in generous quantities
- To carry with him many little gifts; pretty objects that are not very expensive but always available
- To have among his acquaintances a *qawada* (an old woman–pimp)
- He has to be sensitive and capable of shedding tears very easily

Al-Tifashi is obviously more sensitive and sophisticated in his knowledge of women and the politics of desire than Sheikh Nefzawi or Bin Selman. But he shares with them the belief in an active female sexuality. Women in his book are often seeking sexual encounters, and preferably with 'another' partner (the word foreign is used in this context in the text). The women in *Nazhat al-Albab* will use their attributes to reach their target: the jealous one will show her anger, letting the desired man or men hear how much her unfaithful husband had mistreated her, she will incite male desire by acting angry and furious. The desired male cannot resist her and will end up fulfilling her wish: making love to her. The same will happen with all the other types of women. They are different, but they want one thing from men, the sexual act.

These manuals and sources of knowledge end up telling us more about their authors' sexual fantasies and fears than about what they had promised to do: help men understand women's sexuality and perform better their sexual duties. The rumour about the Sexual Chewing Gum reveals similar things about those who are spreading it.

Rumours do not emanate from facts, they are the products of a perception: a rumour is an information that we wish to believe. The wish to believe is always stronger than the quest for credibility says Jean Noel Kapferrer in his excellent book on rumours.[1] What if the internalised fear finds a way to express itself, to relieve itself? 'A rumour that alleviates a deeply rooted sentiment makes the listener less critical' says Kapferer. What if the failure to perform and satisfy women's sexual demands is not caused by the male's shortcoming? What if the danger of sexual encounters and adultery was not the result of the unavoidable mixed nature of contemporary society? What if all these ills had been instigated by an ignominious plot? Then *l'honneur est sauf,* and the anguish is exorcised. Who is better placed to concoct this plot and be successful in its implementation than Israel, the state that has been invincible, has won many wars against the Arabs and has an inflated reputation of efficiency? The transposition is shifted from one male activity (war in the battlefield) to another kind of aggressivity, a biological war (a symbolic castration) that may prove lethal to men's virility and even deny them a progeny. 'The benefits drawn from adhering and being party to a rumour, fully justifies the little consideration given to plausibility' says Kapferrer.

Rumours go as quickly as they come. A few weeks after the big upheaval and the generalised anguish, the whole story was forgotten. It knew neither a solution nor an ending. Could this silent finale be the result of a hidden awareness, born with the emergence of the rumour, that the whole story was a necessary fantasy? Or did the short-lived chewing gum episode evaporated quietly after having accomplished its therapeutic role?

---

1.   Kapferrer, Noel. *Rumeurs, Le Plus Vieux Media Du Monde,* Editions du Seuil 1995

The Egyptian film industry has been more successful in exorcising the feeling of humiliation towards the Israeli supremacy through a totally opposite process: a superwoman, adorned Egyptian film star infiltrates the highest of all Israeli security posts, thanks to her smartness, beauty and courage. Nadia al-Jundi, a very popular actress, invaded Arab cinema and TV screens in the early nineties with her box-office smash hit film *Muhimma fi Tel Aviv* (Mission to Tel Aviv). The film was so successful that it keeps generating sequels and large posters exhibited in the video shops of the remotest corners of the Arab world. Al-Jundi is a victim of the class system in Egypt as well as the unfair laws towards women. Having lost the custody of her child, she turns loose and immoral and ends up as the lover of an Israeli agent in Paris. However, her national feelings and original honesty emerge through at the most crucial time, and she decides to work and use her charms and connections to serve the Egyptian cause. Since she is irresistible, she manages to bring a very high-ranking Israeli security officer to her bedroom, and before making love to him (the spectators do not need to miss the titillating–entertaining bits in the movie) she manages to slip sleeping pills into his drink and to steal the keys of the high security room, where all the strategic Israeli military secrets are kept. She is a hero, a liberated woman who dresses in the sexiest way without losing her dignity or her sense of sacrifice for her country. This fantasy, based on a liberated image of women, drawn and filmed with fun and drama, has survived better as a psychological catharsis than the threatening Sexual Chewing Gum. Instead of chewing gum being slipped in the mouth of Egyptian women, it is an Egyptian lady herself who is slipping some drops into the 'enemy's' mouth. Women's strong sexuality and charms are not attributes created to make impossible demands on men, they are used to a good cause: 'the nationalist struggle'. Women's sexuality is a kind of blessing and it's 'social and national effects' are positive: instead of driving women into an uncontrollable sexual mood – turning them, sometimes, into rapists – active and seductive sexuality is used and displayed for the best of all causes in Nadia al-Jundi's popular thrillers.

Women's sexual powers and desires are no longer a sexual threat for Arab men here, they are a source of power and fun shared by Egyptian males as well as females.

These episodes in the modern life of Arab media are maybe unrelated. I still see through them a chaotic quest for a definition of modern masculinity. Through fears and hopes, anguished images and courageous depiction of 'the new woman', through the revisiting of old sexual manuals and their modern reappropriation, the meaning of masculinity is thrown into question.

Who said it was easy to be a man?

Lola and Farida

She will go through the same routine all right, smiling, showing all her teeth to their 'Come on, Lola'. But tonight her heart's not in it. She's unhappy tonight, like last night and the night before. It could be that the hideous weather or this decaying and decrepit nightclub is getting her down. It's just not up to her art. She knows she's an artist, a professional: the customers never notice when she's pissed.

Her undulations may still be perfect but they've lost the soul that inspired their gracefulness.

Tonight she'll give them the dance of the seven veils again. Tonight she'll perform the dance of Salome: the act that has made her famous in town. She'll arch her arms and swirl the veils round and round until her public sees a rainbow and believes in the skies.

Tonight she'll *act* the dance she once cherished and enjoyed. She once genuinely believed in her art, but this stupid nightclub has gotten on her nerves and slowly eroded her passion.

She used to love it when, through the ritualised curves of her belly and the undulations of her arms, she could draw her public into the mystery of the waves, the bliss of the lyrical and the longings of the flesh. She'd surprise her adoring public with a sudden change of mood, adopting the proud posture of an African queen and following the brisk rhythm of her generous hips.

She liked seducing through her dance, before it became her duty and her business to seduce.

Years ago, when she first came to the city, she was joyous and gay. Her joy spread out generously wherever she went, along with the music generated by the tiny bells around her ankles.

She used to flirt with the dark young musician, through little gestures and signs that only the two of them understood. Theirs was a perfect harmonious duo, a sweet competition between the melody of his flute and the tinkling sound of her anklets. But the dark musician is long gone, and there's a big orchestra now. The musicians care more about the time they will be off than about her quivers, her twirls and the subtle rhythm of her anklets. And why wouldn't they?

Yes, she'll give the customers their money's worth. She'll thrust her hips powerfully up and down a few times, she'll have them come back to watch her and declare loudly that she is still INCREDIBLE, admit that nobody can shake the way she does, that only *she* knows how to make them hold their breath like the trees of a forest awaiting a storm.

She raises her hands and smiles like a star is expected to smile. But her thoughts are not with her public. She's thinking only of one thing: a hot bath and a good night's sleep, and of her day off. On that day she'll dance for her own pleasure, for the love of the music and for herself. She'll shake and undulate through all the fibres of her body and with all her heart. Then she'll be happy for she'll feel genuine and generous. She'll be Farida again, and not Lola the cabaret entertainer.

Photogenic Elections:
Men and Status in Lebanon

There are a few trees left in Beirut, but their branches are no longer to be seen. Large pictures of men hang from them. There are many grey concrete buildings in Lebanon (we call them boxes). They are now quite colourful thanks to the multitude of men's portraits covering their façades. There's a wonderful old building on Sodeco Square: a magnificent skeleton reminding us incessantly of the civil war and its destructive power. It is no longer proudly defying the developers who want to erase it to plague Beirut with another concrete box. It stands there like a desolate past looking helplessly at the ridicule it has to endure: its ornate old columns have been turned into hangers for the pictures of more men, more wishful candidates in the Lebanese parliamentary elections of August 2000.

Walking through the streets of Beirut, driving through the *autostrade* that takes you to the north of the country or going south of the capital, you cannot avoid looking up at these large portraits. You're looking up, but they don't seem to be looking down at you. For,

despite their thick moustaches and their desperate efforts, they fail to emanate a sense of authority, of traditional notability and status, a tool essential to any *zaim*, or leader of men. Perhaps this failure is caused by the multitude of juxtaposed and competing pictures. A notable or a leader should, after all, be easily distinguishable from 'all the others'. But with so many pictures of candidates exhibited and so many candidates wishing to be selected, are the individual and his message (on the rare occasion when there is a message behind the candidacy) not totally lost and submerged? These candidates seem to be projecting their image more than they project their candidacy or express any societal concern. According to Freud, 'The ego is first and foremost a bodily ego ... the projection of a surface.' Are we not witnessing here a festival of bodily egos, a clumsy and adolescent projection of faces? – face (as in façade) as in *wajiha* and *wajih* (*wajih* = notable or man of status; the root of the word in Arabic is the same as 'face'). Could we be looking at an exuberant, Mediterranean explosion of masculine self-presentation? Are these thousands of faces telling us something about Lebanese politics today and the state of democracy in post-war Lebanon?

Elections are not always about politics

'When something is about masculinity, it isn't always about men,' wrote Eve Sedgwick in *Constructing Masculinity*.[1] Looking at the pictures of these male candidates hanging above and around the city, trying to convince us to vote for them in the parliamentary elections, it is tempting to say that in Lebanon, when something is about parliamentary elections, it isn't always about politics. What are these pictures, which have changed the landscape and colour of Lebanese streets, roads and public places, telling us about the state of the country, its real or imagined identities, the anxieties of its citizens and the responsibilities of its leaders and representatives? Do they reflect the changing patterns of power and domination after the trauma of war or are they merely caricatures of its old traditions and uncertain modernity? On the surface, one is tempted to believe that these pictures, often carrying no written message except for the name of the candidate, seem to be saying, 'Look at me, I am here, I am a candidate. Thus I exist. I am not a nobody.'

But this simple message is very revealing and essential to the assessment of the place of the individual in Lebanese society today. This visual message is an outcry for prestige and social status in a small Mediterranean enclave, where concepts like reputation and 'what the neighbours say or think' are still very effective and determining factors in people's behaviour. It is a longing for power that is now reconciled with the idea of being reduced to a much smaller scale (the big matters being increasingly decided upon by non-elected forces and often in the interest of neighbouring countries). This visual exhibition tells us about a society that has not cut its umbilical cord with its old traditions in which its leaders and rulers excelled at negotiating authority, gaining access to benefits and wealth through networks and alliances, be it under Ottoman rule, during the French Mandate or in the post-colonial era.

---

1. Berger, Maurice, Brian Wallis and Simon Watson (eds), *Constructing Masculinity*. New York: Routledge, 1995.

Lebanon as a republican fraternity?

'By the end of the 1920s, three conflicted modes of reconstituted authority emerged and stood in tension with one another, based on paternalistic privilege, republican fraternity and universal democracy' wrote Elizabeth Thompson.[1] It is frightening how this description of Lebanon in the 1920s could be repeated when looking at our candidates and the multitude of expressions they bestow upon us from their studio-made or Photoshop portraits. Paternalism is definitely present in some of these faces – the amiable middle-aged man with the respectable moustache, and just a touch of grey around his temples. The enormous size of these posters aims not only to take our attention away from the multitude of middle-sized portraits, but also to make us feel like children looking up at their father. These same moustaches above a large smile are definitely aiming to project a cool, brotherly demeanour. The candidate may be the son of an old bey, he may be rich, a returning millionaire emigrant, but he's still like us. He seems to be so easy-going that we could give him a tap on the shoulder. Yes, Lebanon is a republican fraternity! Lebanon is indeed a modern country, a universal democracy – look at the portraits: all the candidates are dressed in Western-type suits with austere ties; they're trying to charm us mere mortals into voting for them. They're all presenting themselves as free and autonomous individuals. There's no mention of coalitions, of Syrian veto or the influence of large families on these portraits. Like all photographic pictures, they express an indisputable truth, but not all of it. Perhaps we can try to read what the pictures don't say. The following are statements made by 'citizens' about the elections in August:

People argue, they make cynical remarks, but they end up voting. They will vote in their village or town of origin. They may have lived

---

1. Thompson, Elizabeth, *Colonial Citizens, Republican Rights, Paternal Privilege, and Gender in French Syria and Lebanon*. New York: Columbia University Press, 2000.

and worked for ages in a town where their parents were not born, it does not matter. This system has hindered the development of Lebanese democracy and tied the individual to his or her family's allegiances and concerns. When an engineer, a teacher or a state employee goes to vote for a candidate born in the same place as his father and father's father, the concerns, hopes and frustrations of the large family are more at stake than the decisions and policies of the candidate and his influence on the parliament.

The various tales of masculinity

The photo-portraits present a large array of masculine traits, from the wise intellectual behind professional glasses, to the reassuring smile of a friendly candidate. One candidate in the Bekaa Valley decided to present himself doing aerobic exercises in his garden! If these photographs tell us something about men and politics in Lebanon, it is of conflicting images or, more accurately, of juxtaposed value systems and of a democracy torn between some of its rooted traditions and its congenital infirmities. They speak of men who call for your democratic vote while giving in to elitism and dictatorial impositions. The few female candidates hardly change anything in the male panorama that dominates the country. It is significant that the written messages, when available, are as insipid as possible: *Ma bi sih illa as-Sahih* (Only the right thing is right!) is the slogan under the Prime Minister's electoral portrait. Sometimes the messages betray a ridiculous paranoia: the slogan of an incognito candidate tells us 'Don't be afraid, I am with you.' Many large posters on the road to Tripoli contain different landscapes of Lebanon, thanks to Photoshop techniques, as backgrounds to the candidate's portrait. One rich immigrant raised slogans calling – out of the blue and in contradiction to his Clark Gable postures – for women's emancipation. Lebanon, in this new landscape, seems to be preparing for a carnival rather than a new parliament. The words of the poet Nadia Tueni come to mind: 'My country tells me ... do take me seriously.' In order to feel better about it all, I recall the days, those terrible days, when my country was covered in pictures of martyrs and when the red colour of blood was predominant. Then I look at the pictures of our candidates and indulge in a little bemused smile.

Lamia

Who is in control after all?

Lamia was different and intriguing. I cannot tell what made her seem different from all of us and why I believed her to be absolutely inaccessible. Her smile was more discreet than ours, her lips more generous and her haircut more radical than was conceivable in those days. Her cautious expression and her hesitant phrases enhanced the sense of mystery that accompanied her rare words.

Lamia was transformed on the basketball field. There, her steps were nimble and her body moved with the happiness of a wild deer. On the basketball field Lamia looked wonderfully svelte and powerful. She would run past any other player, jump higher than the tallest girl in the team.

I will always cherish the day I met Lamia for the first time outside our school. She was swimming in the sea, diving into the water with a sudden extension of her legs, reappearing swiftly to breathe deeply before holding her nose with her wet fingers and diving again.

Emerging from the water, she saw me standing perplexed and

hesitant on the shore, testing the temperature of the water with my foot. She waved, inviting me to join her, laughing cheerfully at my cautiousness, laughing through her glittery pink lips. The freshness of the sea had a miracle effect on Lamia. I decided that, maybe, after all Lamia was a girl like all other girls with more, much more stamina. The games she insisted on playing had all something to do with reaching impossible targets and limits. 'Can you count up to fifty underwater?' 'Can you swim to the raft keeping your legs crossed?' Can you ... Can you? I felt I could attempt the impossible, now that this shadowy figure had turned into a little girl I could have fun with.

The day when Lamia waved to me on the beach marked the beginning of a long and tumultuous friendship. I used to dread the Sundays when we would go to the mountains to visit my grandparents instead of the beach, and would beg my parents not to take me with them, but to leave me with my older sisters in Beirut. I thanked God vehemently for the fact that Lamia's family did not have a summer residence. Gradually, my initial fears that she would withdraw again into the quiet, inaccessible girl I knew at school began to subside, as did the memory of her silent and austere pink lips.

Strawberry flavours. Shy menstrual dark drops. Faint crimson teenage dreams. Early morning cyclamen fields. Auburn hopes and wishful thoughts.

That summer remains enchanted in my memory. It had a lightness, a happiness that we took for granted. Everything happened on the beach, and there we both turned into dark, talkative little girls. Nothing disturbed us, or only a few things which did not seem important at the time, but now when I remember that blissful summer they cast a shadow across my memory: sometimes, when I felt lazy and didn't want to compete with pirouettes and at breath-holding records underwater, Lamia's face turned stiff with anger and I knew that she hated me; she despised me in my 'idleness'.

Now, some twenty years later, Lamia is still svelte and energetically thin. Her allure is more like that of my older daughter, Nora, who has just turned fifteen. I cannot help feeling like a rather plump mother whose daughter will always be firm and agile. My daughter is more like Lamia, at least she tries to imitate her, in the way she walks, the way she dresses, and in the reproachful glances she throws at me when I leave home without any make-up on or with my shoes unpolished. For nobody ever thinks of Lamia but as the woman with the rich rouge, a colour that she wears on her lips defiantly. Even me! I find it difficult to remember the pale adolescent girl who confided quietly about her family and her pains. Now that I am saying this, I realise that while Lamia told me plenty of things about her brothers, and quite a bit about her father (who was often on business abroad) she hardly ever mentioned her mother. When she did, it always had something to do with what she was allowed and not allowed to do.

Last week Nora had a temper tantrum and God did her expression remind me of Lamia's angry face on the beach! She wanted us to move back to central London, and it was pointless trying to explain to her that we would never have been able to afford a nice large house if we hadn't come to live in Greenford. How could we have afforded a four-bedroom house in the centre of London? 'Surely you wouldn't have wanted to share your room with one of your brothers?' I felt desperate. So much sacrifice, so much effort and my daughter never seems to be happy. Richard, my husband, is never much help either. He shies away from such discussions. He takes a book from the shelf, and retracts into silence and more abstract concerns.

'She's right, what are you doing playing at middle-class English suburbia? You're not doing anything for yourself and you're turning into a narrow-minded fat housewife.'

This was Lamia's response, no doubt blurted out through her confident rouge lips, when I asked her advice on the phone. Actually, I wasn't seeking advice but comfort and encouragement. Lamia could be cruel. Cruel, blunt and unfair. I felt hurt. That was a terrible thing to say. All right, I've put on weight, but I have had three children. She can afford the luxury of keeping fit, or reading the *London Review of Books* and *Wallpaper* 'because there is no such thing as popular or high culture', she likes to declare with her nauseating self-assurance. She has no responsibility but to herself and her own elegance and charm. She is so much in control that her heart is hardening and her tenderness is getting lost between her achievements and her scarlet glamour.

'I am happy as I am,' I said in a voice that tried to hide its shaking. All doors seem to be closing on me. First my unhappy daughter and now Lamia, my last resort for comfort, spitting cruel words in my face. I wanted to scream at her, insult her, tell her that Richard was right to call her an irritating shrew, that she lacked warmth, and that she was not slim but skinny and unfeminine. But as always, since that summer that started it all, I held back my tears, strangled my frustration and felt ashamed of my creeping jealousy of Lamia.

Red pain. Red anger. Cheeks burning with brown fury. Flushes of frustrations soaked in malt vinegar. Rotten beetroots. Stains of rouge-baiser *blood.*

I hate myself for envying Lamia. Whenever I feel that way, I rush to the mirror to convince myself that we are just different. Complementary. My lips are discreet while hers are scarlet and aggressive. My hips are round and heavy, because they carried my three beautiful children. I think that my strength is settling more securely on the ground, the heavier I become, the more stable my home and family are. Lamia's power, on the other hand, extends vertically towards the sky; it reaches other horizons through her lean stretched body. Lamia always reaches further, extends the limits of things, and she seems to have wilfully extended her body above us all. When I feel ashamed of myself, I try to remind myself that I am the one who encouraged my daughter to become like her. When she marries, I want my daughter to divorce her husband if he disappoints her, as Lamia did three years ago. I want my daughter to be independent and active and successful the way Lamia is. So what right do I have to be jealous?

Lamia came to visit, on the Sunday after our upsetting telephone conversation. She didn't let us know she was coming. She didn't apologise. Her curly black hair and smiling white face showed up behind a huge bouquet of mimosas and red carnations, which she held firmly in her left hand. Look, she said, handing me the book she was holding in her other hand. *A She Front.* This was her way of telling me that she wasn't going to apologise, but that she did still value my opinion, and that she would love to discuss the book with me, just like we used to do at school and at university, I thought to myself with a touch of nostalgia. I had read reviews of *A She Front.* I was sceptical; I usually ignore the latest bestseller. Nowadays the media churns out a new literary genius every week, 'the greatest author since Joyce or Proust'.

'Thanks,' I said, 'that's very nice of you. You should have waited for the paperback. You've read the book, I know. Don't you think it would have been better for a more subtle and literary writer to tackle the subject of sexual harassment? I have nothing against the success of *Ladies Park*, but this success doesn't give Salem licence to explore the so-called women's want for power.'

'You mean only a woman and an academic feminist should be allowed to touch such holy subjects?'

Lamia said these words with a playful flicker of the iris and a little flirtatious smile. Her lips were brighter and redder than usual She was asking me not to take her remark very seriously. She was trying her best not to be aggressive.

'No, but seriously! This is a male fantasy or at best a transposition. Women do not confuse power with sexuality the way men do, sorry! Some men do. A male boss, when he approaches a secretary sexually, is asserting his superiority and confirming his hierarchical position. A woman who reaches the top sphere of her profession is constantly trying to establish an appropriate distance from her male subordinates and this often requires a conscious effort at desexualising her environment.'

'How do you know about that? It is only very recently that we heard of trials involving sexual harassment by men. And women general managers are a pretty recent phenomenon. The lust for power knows no sex. Really, I prefer women who are upfront about it to those who hide it. What I loathe is hypocrisy.'

'Wait a minute. I thought we were different. We wanted to create a world with new values. One in which the hierarchies established by male values would disappear.'

'Yeah?' Lamia moved into fighting mood, her torso leaning in my direction, her ruby lips forming a sarcastic sneer. 'Who says so, Mrs Ghandi or Mrs Thatcher?'

Lamia is always ahead of me. She keeps coming out with new ideas, conclusions, just when I've assimilated the last stage she introduced me to. I can't go so fast, I DO NOT WANT TO. Not when she twists her lips and raises her voice. I can't think unless the tone is smooth and comforting.

'Oh my God, I forgot to turn the gas down under the pan.'

I rushed into the kitchen. Lamia picked up a magazine that was lying on the table and retreated into it. She understands now that it's time to end our discussion. She wants to make things better between us, and is making a real effort not to force her arguments further.

This is Lamia, I said to myself, back in my kitchen. She hates what she calls hypocrisy. When she utters this word, I know that she is upset, so the best thing is to let go. The image of her mother sticks to this word hypocrisy: Sitt Selma.

Now in a way I feel sorry for Sitt Selma. I disliked her thoroughly at the beginning, but often nowadays I find myself trying to mellow Lamia and push her, though I never succeed, into a more tolerant attitude towards her mother.

I glance through the window and see Lamia relaxed reading the magazine with her legs stretched in front of her, her heavy black boots resting on the edge of the round garden table. How different she is from her mother. When Sitt Selma was our age, she had already begun to stoop, wear grey suits and speak in a low voice. The more Sitt Selma behaved as if she didn't want anything for herself on this earth, the more my fear of her grew and disturbed me. Is this why Lamia always dresses so extravagantly? Is it because she needs to destroy the example of her mother that she keeps changing lovers, and always chose married men? I used to think she liked a challenge, but now I'm more and more convinced that with married men she can keep her Sundays to herself, and never repeat her mother's words: 'On Sunday. When did I ever do something on a Sunday which was not for the sake of you and the children?' Or again: 'I will only rest on my deathbed. I am not like these other women, watching their looks and cosseting themselves. I have no demands or time to myself. Everything is for him' – meaning Sayed Adel, Lamia's father – 'and for you.' Actually Sitt Selma was everything but a passive victim. Always staring at her feet as if she was too modest to raise her head, she still managed to interfere in every little detail and dictate every choice made by every single member of her family. She was mean and cruel towards Latifa, the old maid who was related to her and most probably younger than her. She kept calling her 'the old witch' who was 'eating, sleeping and profiting from my generosity and kindness'.

'*Hatha min ghadab Allah.*' Sitt Selma loved this phrase; she would say it whenever somebody had a problem, a tragedy or an accident. Her one and only explanation: 'It is God's wrath falling on those deserving.' She would invite Sitt Samira, and her neighbour, the newly wed Olga, over in the morning, prepare a narghile, order Latifa around, put on her new grey suit and get all nervous about breaking the tragic news. If Madame Angel's son had been taken to hospital with pneumonia it was because Madame Angel had been busy putting on her make-up, and trying to look young and attractive, and had neglected him. If Suraya's husband had treated her badly by getting drunk and seeing other women, it was because Suraya did not pray enough and submitted to her husband's every whim. One way or another, Sitt Selma would pour all her venom onto other women, then look with her modest smile towards Sitt Samira and say, 'God preserve us from those miseries, after all we are sinners, and most probably I am not doing enough for my family.'

Sitt Samira, red-faced between a puff of narghile and another slice of cake, would disagree loudly, 'Oh don't say that. You are a saint, Sitt Selma! They don't make women like you any more.'

Bitter aubergines. Sour grapes of envy. Bitter blood running through veins of pain. Smashed old pomegranate. Lifeless shades of vampire smiles.

During these Saturdays at home, Lamia and I would listen through the door of the salon, which adjoined the drawing room they used for such special *matinées*. Lamia would mimic her mother's face while she was gossiping about somebody or her constant pleas for God's mercy. She'd first adopt the pose of the Virgin Mary, loving and shy, and then she'd stand up and start moving her lips faster and faster while her eyes scanned the room with a vindictive dark expression. Then she'd put her hands together, look at the sky asking for God's pardon and immediately look sideways to make sure that everybody saw her in this humble position. This is when we would fall on the floor laughing until Latifa would rush out and ask us to be less noisy, for we were her responsibility and would be punished for our bad behaviour. Sitt Selma never did anything noisy or nasty herself; she would get her husband to do it for her. Or so Lamia said.

'She used to wait for him to come back from work, then she'd lock herself with him in the room for hours, weeping to him about all her problems and the misery she was enduring because of whoever. He would come out of the room absolutely furious and shout at Latifa, threatening to throw her out on the street, or into an old people's home, or he'd punish us by locking us in, or taking some treat away from us. Once he had the grocer, Saleh, throw out the delivery boy, who was less than fourteen years old because he hadn't responded to Mum's orders swiftly enough.'

Lamia never blamed her father; she definitely blamed it all on her mother's 'ruses and mischievous plots'. Power is in everything and everywhere, she kept repeating when she left her parents' home. 'I will be strong and straightforward, I will do what I want to do myself. I will take responsibility for my decisions.' And so she did. I have to grant her that. She looks so powerful. She *is* powerful. She knows no fear, or perhaps that is the easiest way to describe her unnerving ,unsettling freedom.

I was so deep in thought I hadn't noticed Nora coming out of her room. I heard their two voices debating. Lamia was arguing with my daughter. I wish I could hear what they were saying. I think I know and I am grateful to Lamia. She was on my side. All my anger melted into gratitude. Again Lamia is teaching me that envy is the worst emotion. Lamia always defends women. She draws her strength from this solidarity; she draws it from the negative image of Sitt Selma. How many times did we hear Sitt Selma saying to her audience, 'What did he see in her? She isn't pretty, or rich, or even from a very good family.' In any match, Sitt Selma would always find the man better than the woman. She would spit out all her negative remarks about the woman and her family and then look saintly again and say, 'But I only wish them happiness, I only have good thoughts towards everybody.'

Nora came to the kitchen, she kissed me and said, 'I'm sorry, Lamia is right, if I wish to live in London I'd better find my own means to do it. Lamia says freedom is risky and difficult. She's right.'

'Yes, darling,' I said, kissing her back.

I felt my eyes betraying me, moistening as I struggled to say, 'Don't take it as hard on you as Lamia does.' I rushed to the cupboard, took out a tray and started to prepare a pot of Turkish coffee. Our faithful ritual, our way of saying we are still Lebanese. Drinking tea would feel like a betrayal, and even Richard has learned to praise 'our' coffee in front of his friends. When he gave up tea I felt it as a confirmation of love and faithfulness to me.

R like in red and in refugee. Orange and violet nostalgia the sound of melancholic voices. Calls from a lost tanned past. Clear Darjeeling liquid missed like impossible hopes.

Lamia didn't come round or telephone for three weeks. I was beginning to get worried. On the answering machine her voice sounded to me more and more anxious in tone. It is your own anxiousness, Richard commented reassuringly. 'You misguidedly think that Lamia is such a goddess that when she is not there, the world must be crumbling.'

There was a trace of bitterness in his voice. I tried to comfort him with a kiss, but we both knew that nothing would wipe that trace away. Still, we were both hoping Lamia would show up. This was on a Friday evening and we settled our unease by watching a mediocre detective movie on TV after the two boys had gone to sleep and Nora had put on her headphones, retracting into the world of rap.

9 a.m. on Saturday morning, just as I was sipping my first cup of coffee, I heard her parking her car. I rushed down so as not to interrupt Richard reading his newspaper and, moreover, so that I could be with her first, alone. Lamia looked different, tired with the deep lines of sleepless nights under her eyes. She looked gorgeous, though, in her dishevelled state. Her twisted smile came to her mouth with difficulty.

'Everything is going in the wrong direction,' she offered as an explanation. 'They gave the job to Allen. He doesn't deserve it', she said, 'and I wanted this post. He is an ass-licker and that's what they want. Latifa wants to live with me, because my mother is threatening to send her to a wretched, cheap, filthy old people's home. Huh! Solly, whom I've been seeing for a year now, says unless I marry him it's all over. He left his wife and family last month. Nothing is right.'

She sat down in the living room, while I rushed to pour her a cup of my morning coffee. When I came back, her eyes were closed. I watched her for a moment sitting with her legs slightly apart, her hands in her lap and her lips pressed tight. She looked like her mother. Bitter and unhappy. I never wanted to see her like that; I never wanted to see in her features any of her mother's legacies. I felt desperate. I could feel sorry for Sitt Selma, but I needed to admire Lamia. Selfishly, I said to myself, 'In a moment Lamia will get up, look strong and wonderful and win.'

Lamia opened her eyes, looked at me and said, 'You know, I really envy you. You are in control, and me, I'm always trying. Anyway, I've made up my mind, I'm going to give Solly the flick, he's far too demanding. I'm going to take my editor-in-chief to a fair pay tribunal for giving the job to a man who deserves it less than me. And somehow I will find a solution for Latifa. Get dressed, come on, why don't we go out and have a picnic.'

I went up to dress and I felt happy. I rushed to Nora's room and took her most aggressive rouge, 'Scelerat', and applied it confidently to my lips. They looked vivid and assertive. Yes, I am in control, and they all end up coming back to me, to my home. I am the point of stability. They would feel lost without me. Even Lamia.

Lisa My Eager Neighbour

My neighbour Lisa is a dear. That is what I felt as soon as I moved into my new home. How could we ever manage without Lisa? I kept thinking to myself. Like all normal human beings, particularly those who originate from countries where *fawda* (anarchy) rules, I dread filling out forms. But Lisa has no problem filling out forms: forms about tree-trimming, forms about parking regulations, forms about satellite dishes and cable aerials and their interference with the aesthetics of the neighbourhood, forms about garbage retrieval. I'm not even talking of the other billion forms that find their way into our mailboxes when we have to redecorate the façade of our house or attend to some of those familiar little English leaks. Lisa, wonderful, dynamic Lisa is always ready and willing to respond studiously on behalf of all the occupants of this small building, which looks so cosy and easygoing to passers-by. Lisa does it perfectly; she knows the vocabulary and the proper expressions as well as the mentality and wishes of the bureaucrat who is going to check the form and file it. Moreover, what seems to be a hellish task for us seems to be a mere little *passe-temps* for Lisa. I have even noticed that she fills out these forms with a smile; actually I would venture to say with some pleasure. Whenever there's any little business concerning the building and its maintenance, Lisa appears miraculously, full of enthusiasm. You could be tempted to say that the problems in our building bring happiness and exhilaration to Lisa. Lucky us, I kept telling myself. Neighbours are important, but in my case, the existence of Lisa was a gift from God.

But even God, it seems, gives nothing for nothing. My optimism in life was shortlived. I should have known better than to believe that my happiness was going to be gratis and eternal. Ha! The lovely, energetic smile of our volunteer slowly started to lose its charm. For she didn't appear only when there were forms to fill, but also started to look eagerly for new ones.

'Did you receive the new council tax forms?' she'd ask me on her way out to work.

And if I hadn't, Lisa would turn sulky and irritated, her blue eyes saddened by the lack of opportunity. Yes, Lisa has a regular job. I couldn't believe it at first for she was always there, waiting for me on my way out of the flat, receiving me on the doorstep on my way back, always carrying some important news about the building and its needs, multiple endless needs! Not only did Lisa fill in the forms but she also needed to speak about them, like an adolescent who had enjoyed a party and was eager to speak about it at length with her girlfriends afterwards. I started to believe that she had invented some of these forms. And the more she spoke about the building the more I saw her eyes turn from blue to grey and her body thinning into a vertical line. Oh Lisa! Yes, nice Lisa, helpful Lisa, but ...

My coming out and in of my house is no longer an easy matter. I cannot remember a day when I walked through the gate without Lisa rushing to me with some problem concerning our common 'property'. Nothing that can be solved or discussed in a few minutes is ever on the agenda. Oh no, not for such important matters as the colour of the outside light, or the fees of the cleaners or ... These are of the utmost importance for Lisa and conversations can easily drag on for an hour.

I started using some tactics, like never leaving home without running, to show that I'm hopelessly late for my next appointment. Whenever I needed to go through the gate, I showed up carrying heavy bags, and leaning theatrically to one side under their weight to show that I ought to deposit them immediately if I wanted to avoid lumbago. But none of these tactics were successful in deterring Lisa. I used all possible strategies, but she kept winning the battle, until the day when, in utter desperation, I told her, 'Lisa, please do as you please. I agree with every decision you make concerning the building. Please don't consult me. You are the best judge.' I acted like a defeated general in a battle. I surrendered totally in order to walk peacefully through my front door. You'd think Lisa would be satisfied with that. But no, not at all. Her smile turned into a nasty smirk and she held a thick pile of forms – each no doubt hiding a hundred questions – and said, 'If you don't care for your interests why should I?'

Lisa was standing in front of the building like a victorious general who's been deprived of celebrating his victory. I looked at the pile of papers and realised that I was in deep trouble. It is either these or Lisa, I thought to myself, and I retracted immediately. Since then, I'm resigned to spending more time near the gate of my home chatting with Lisa and showing great interest in the multiple needs of our 'property'. I've tried to change my schedule, come at different times of the day, but she's always there, waiting for me.

She is a master of this kind of warfare. I dream of travelling to some desert island while we're standing there talking, where people sleep under the sky, with no roofs over their heads that need painting or repairing and where paper hasn't yet been discovered.

Dear, dear Lisa! Your eagerness and efficiency are turning me into a utopian dreamer.

Il est Interdit d'Interdire

It is banned to ban. How I loved this phrase. I was young when I heard it the first time and I stood by it absolutely like youth stands by its principles. I am less young today and I still try to scream loudly 'It is banned to ban!' But over the years I've found the absolutism of this phrase challenged, not only by those who raise their scissors and those in power, but by people like you and me, people who in principle abhor repression and the amputation of creativity. After all the difficulty with the slogan is that it includes the word *interdit*, 'banned'. This is why I thank *Freemuse* for the opportunity to think deeper about the question of censorship, to understand why people like to muzzle other voices, erase words and burn books instead of turning their eyes, blocking their ears, turning a page or going for a walk when they dislike a tune or some words.

I don't want to waste these few precious moments on the most common and abject reasons that lie behind the scissors and the muzzles of the censors: the preservation of power by dictators, totalitarian regimes, loud racists, fanatics and the likes. We all know about them, they do not try to hide their motives; they are afraid of freedom and believe only in their freedom to impose one speech, one colour and one tune, the one that keeps them in power, and the only one that should be heard or seen because they enjoy hearing it and seeing it themselves. I am not going to speak of the Inquisition and its fathers who tried to censor even the souls of people and mould them to serve the needs of their church, nor speak of the Nazis who not only banned music they considered degenerate because it did not fit their understanding of melody, but also banned art created by Jews and Gypsies, people they decided to dehumanise. I will not speak of those fundamentalists who want to ban music as such, for they have more chance of succeeding if they try to stop birds from singing. No, what I would like to address this evening, and what I would like to learn more about during this symposium, are the more discreet forms of censorship, the invisible ones, the ones that also lie behind 'good intentions'. I would like to learn from our debates why I hear many decent people suddenly calling for the banning of this book, or that image or this song. I want us to find out why, when we find a song offensive – be it for sexual, political or even aesthetic reasons – we ask 'How do they allow people to publish this?' And I am saying this because I know that this reaction is spontaneous, humanly spontaneous and that even people who insist that 'Il est interdit d'interdire' find themselves saying, 'This shouldn't be allowed,' instead of saying, 'I don't want to listen to this.' I would like to understand because none of us are immune to falling under the spell of banning as a solution in difficult times, or when we think that our children are threatened.

Let me be more explicit. Listen to the following lyrics:

Slap hips, support domestic violence
Beat your bitch's ass while your kids stare in silence

This is Eminem – Slim Shady.
Another tune, a few decades earlier:

> *J'ai envie de violer des femmes*
> *De les forcer a m'admirer,*
> *Envie de boire toutes leurs larmes et de disparaitre en fumee.*

> (I feel like raping women
> to make them love me
> To drink their tears etc ...)

Michel Sardou. The same Michel Sardou not only needed to humiliate women but Arabs as well:

> *Ils ont du petrole, mais ils n'ont que ça.*
> (They have oil, but that's all they have.)

Recently, very recently, Capleton, the Jamaican reggae star, had two concerts cancelled in Britain and in France. He'd been singing loud and proud:

> All Boogaman and sodomites fi get killed ... Burn out a Queer,
> Blood out a queer.

I translate it as this: All faggots should get killed; burn a queer, kill a queer. You do, I'm sure, find these words disgusting. So should these songs be banned?

Should we ask the radio stations to only broadcast them when the children have gone to bed? Should we have joined the feminist and the gay pride movement's demonstration against the right of these singers to express their hatred?

If I cannot dismiss the legitimate outrage felt by the attacked groups through these words, I still cannot see myself joining the call for the banning of these songs or concerts. Because I deeply believe in the freedom of expression, and if I ask for the freedom to express my own views and tastes, I should have the courage to let others express their own views, however ugly or hurtful or painful they are to my eyes and ears.

I know that some here will ask, 'What about racism? What about hate speech calling for murder?'

I know! I'm here to listen and be convinced that words can lead to violence. I'm here to find out how we can have an enlightened law fighting racism and discrimination while defending freedom of expression, all expressions. It is not easy, but this is a challenge worth facing.

Let us not shy away from some disturbing dilemmas: if hate speech truly can result in violent action, can we honestly feel secure when we say NO to any kind of silencing or censorship? The case of David Pallister, the eighteen-year-old who battered to death a man who was sleeping rough in a shelter, is revealing. Pallister claimed that he acted out the brutal lyrics of Eminem. Two months ago the judge in Newcastle, where the crime took place, sentenced him to life imprisonment. Millions of kids listen to Eminem and they don't act on the lyrics or take them at face value. I do agree with the court's conclusion that expressing and acting are not synonymous; they are not in the same category. If the image of something and this something were directly related how come many of us who grew up watching the cartoons of Tom and Jerry didn't become awfully violent? Remember how much bashing and kicking and head-banging the poor cat went through while we were laughing and enjoying ourselves?

Remember Serge Gainsbourg? Censored for his song *Je vais et je viens*, or his ironic remake of *La Marseillaise*. Remember *Relax* by Frankie Goes to Hollywood? They were banned not that long ago. Looking at MTV or our own Arabic music channels, they sound like kindergarten chants nowadays. When I was a teenager in Beirut two songs were banned by the then Prime Minister: *Riji ala Ishu hal Usfur* and *Ya mon Cher Qu'est-ce que nous allons faire, Bayn al-Thaleth wel Rabea Inqata' Fina al-Ascenseur* (the lift was stuck between the third and fourth floor). What did we all do then: rush to get a tape or a record of these forbidden *Ta'atee'* (popular kitsch songs)?

To those who believe that censorship works I will repeat the famous Arab saying, *Kul Mamnou' Marghoub* (All that is banned is desired). In the Al Saqi bookshop in London many people walk in and ask, 'Where are the banned books?' And it's always a problem, because no bookshop can have a banned section next to the history, fiction and dictionaries sections!

What I'm trying to say is that banning as censorship doesn't really work. It's becoming almost impossible in the age of Internet and mass tourism and cheap flights to really suppress a book, a song or an image. This kind of censorship only makes it easier for those who are privileged, well off or well connected to have access. It makes the life of those who are not connected narrower and brings a new discrimination between the haves and the have nots.

Censorship hasn't disappeared. It is unfortunately still with us, in us: would we call the quotas imposed for a while on the French radio to encourage the national language and music censorship or would we call it encouragement? When most giant record chains are putting small shops out of business, while at the same time promoting their own labels, is this invisible censorship or just the way capitalism is going? Are we immune, however courageous we are, to the most pernicious type of censorship: self-censorship? Shouldn't we fight the glorification of consensus and its rewards, the attraction of social acceptance in order to free our creativity from all constraints and fears? Is it our business here to interfere with people's psyches? Again, please let us discuss, for the answers are all but simple.

I'll leave with a baggage of questions and a big homage to the great Billie Holiday, whose songs were not banned but who was censored in the ugliest way. She could sing whatever she wanted, but in the South, in those segregated days, she was asked to take the service lift, the servants' lift, because of the colour of her skin. It is racism that should be outlawed. Words and tunes as such don't kill; weapons kill.

The Jazz Club

The thing about it all is that the atmosphere is soothingly dark and warm. A damp breeze catches you before you reach your seat. A brief, ephemeral chill that the music and the whisky will soon take care of. You know it; you are here for it. You are here for the physical caress of a multitude of sounds, the inhalation of the air through the brass and its expiration, the friction of wood on skin and the ice cubes falling to the bottom of the glass, just before the liquid drips deliciously over them.

Hush! Your hands squeeze your neighbour's arm just above the elbow. No more words. No need to say, explain, describe or comment any longer. The musicians are on stage; they feel their instruments and adjust them. No more words. You're hanging on to your chair, your eyes are following the golden, black and glittering movement of the instruments and the grave faces of their musicians – their magicians.

Suddenly the sound emerges, powerful, drawn deeply from within. Pure like the voice of one single reality, it cuts through the smoky room like a stone breaks the blue water.

I can see him bending back. Only his legs are visible under the huge saxophone. The notes erupt from the round womb of the instrument; they are delivered towards the ceiling and turned into a flowing melody that will soon break into sobs and cries like the anguished complaints of a newborn expelled from his mother's womb.

From the dark suit, the bronzed skin and the tenor sax emanates a full-blooded sound.

The musician cruises through his solo with proud ease, he carries his melody into an arrogant scream. Now he retreats slowly, carrying his tune with him to the corner of the stage where he extinguishes it in the midst of our applause. He sweeps his mouth and approaches the ashtray where he's left a lit cigarette.

The bass player has stepped forward and is already playing when our *yeahs* filter into silence and our hands reach for our drinks, holding the cool glasses to soothe their red heat.

The murmur of the bass is delightful and is welcomed like the visit of a close friend after the excitements of a passionate encounter. The bass moans: *yeah*, I'm warm, relaxing, almost too civilised, but I could be wild if I wanted. I'm often passionate, just pay more attention to my strings and my deep notes and you will see how I could be a star in my own way. Yes, the brass solo finishes amidst applause, but it's nothing compared to the gasping reaction and the screams that had celebrated the saxophone.

The saxophonist steps in, strong, imposing. He immediately breaks into a thousand short blows. The notes on his horn are swinging, screaming, sobbing, fighting to get free and getting freed all right. We desperately hang on to these notes. We let them invade us, stick to our hot skin, haunt our stretched nerves.

The magic embraces us and sinks deep into the smoke, the drinks and our souls.

Edith Piaf

Vous les beaux mâles je vous ai longtemps aimés, je vous ai pleurés, collés de frissons, suppliés, oubliés, traînés comme de drôles d'erreurs et chantés comme seuls les dieux savent le faire.

Vous les belles et les filles de joies, les adorées et les mal-aimées, je vous ai fredonné des airs à vous faire piétiner le chagrin. Je vous ai gueulé des passions à vous faire décrocher la lune. Je vous ai chanté des je t'aime par milliers, des je t'aime à vous étourdir, à vous faire chialer à coup de violons et d'accordéons.

Allez, venez. Venez vous assoir à ma table, venez vous blottir dans mes airs, vous accrocher à ma voix, vous frotter contre mes pleurs, et vous saoûler de mes mots d'amour. Ces mots banals comme la vie, ces mots de tous les jours que je sais si bien vous dire. Venez, puisez dans mes désirs, mes folies, mes détresses. Je les chante si bien ces mots – des mots tant dis et redis – ces pour toujours que je vous lance à pleins poumons, qui me rentrent dans là peau par là-bas, par la-haut, qui me montent la fièvre à la gorge et lui fichent des cordes de tigresse. Mes chansons, y'en a pour tous, pours les aimés, les délaissés les va-nus-pieds. Pour ceux qui m'ont fait tant souffrir et ceux que j'ai vite oubliés. Pour les Johnny, pour les beaux mecs, pour mon soldat et les fiers milords.

Toi mon boxeur qui a su si bien m'aimer, me faire frémir avec tes baisers dans mon cou, avec tes doigts secs et lents sur ma peau, tes gestes tendres et tes pauvres promesses. Pour toi j'aurais été jusqu'au bout du monde, je me serais faite teindre en blonde. Toi et moi on s'comprenait bien, va. On avait, chacun à sa façon, vendu notre corps pour pouvoir manger. La vie t'a arraché a moi. Chienne de vie. Sans toi je ne suis rien, sans toi je cherche parmi la foule, desemparée, désespérée. Sans toi je cherche un autre corps pour le caresser de mes mots, pour me réchauffer l'âme. Car finalement, finalement, c'est la passion qui me fait vibrer, qui me fait chanter. C'est la musique qui me fait gueuler ces mots tendres, ces mots insensés, ces mots cruels qui vous flanquent le chagrin au ventre et vous donnent envie d'aimer à en crever.

C'est drôle, je chante toujours la pauvre môme, moi qui ne fait plus les rues depuis longtemps. Moi qui ai lancé tant de mecs sur scène. Y'en a qui m'ont oubliée dés que la scène leur a souri, mais après tout j'm'en fous pas mal, il peut m'arriver n'importe quoi, ca m'est égal, j'ai ma voix pour chanter les peines et les joies, j'ai la rue où j'ai grandi et qui ne m'abandonnera pas, j'ai mon public pour chanter à plein coeur, à pleine gorge. J'ai vous pour m'applaudir, j'ai vous pour m'aimer. Aimez moi.

Monuments for an Age without Heroes

When we think of monuments we think of history, battles, impossible achievements; we think of great symphonies, of victories and defeats. This is why our age has problems with monuments. They are always controversial. Nobody likes destroying big sculptures of 'heroes' that have imposed themselves at one point or another on history, and since we cannot, in our modernity, declare a truth without having its contrary thrown in our face, we are weary of statues. We are the generation who will not be immortalised as statues. It's rare for those who are going to be eternalised in bronze to resist immortality. But there are exceptions. The German writer Günter Grass refused to have his statue erected in Gdańsk, his town of birth. The story goes as follows: the people of Gdańsk wanted to celebrate this great writer, this Nobel prizewinner who originated in their town, in the way people of greatness are usually celebrated, by erecting a statue in the centre of the town. They then planned to ask him to come and lift the veil to inaugurate it, thus giving the great man his due. But Grass is a man of today, a man who has developed his convictions through the turmoil of the Second World War and Europe's dark modern ages. Grass grew up in a typical modest building in this Europe that is limitlessly contradictory; a Europe that has realised, in its better moments, that heroes can be dangerous and that their memory can come with a bitter aftertaste; that the bigger the monuments are for these idols, the further we stray from democracy.

Grass grew up in this modest building that is still inhabited by modest families in Gdańsk. Grass's building had no toilets. To this day its inhabitants have to go out to relieve themselves, often in cold and harsh weather conditions. Grass apologised to the town organisers and declined the invitation. He wanted the money that was to be spent on the statue to be spent instead on building toilets for each flat in the building.

How can one not love Grass for this good and humane gesture? He at least demands respect, if not love. But since we are modern, we immediately realise that things aren't that simple. How can we conceive of a world without the Elgin Marbles or the Eiffel Tower? How can we communicate through continents and ages without these monumental symbols? They are, after all, big and tall and so noticeable by many and from far away, and they acquire a shared acknowledgment. Can we imagine Trafalgar Square without Nelson's statue? Or do we care about Nelson's terrible battles when we tell our friends who are visiting London that we shall meet in Trafalgar Square?

The First Casualty of this War was not Truth

Contrary to the media adage, the first casualty of this war was not truth.

The truth can be curtailed nowadays, and this has already happened. But it is extremely difficult to victimise it altogether. The first casualty of this war is not truth but human rights.

Not long ago, during the Clinton era, it looked as if human rights were going to be seriously recognised as a universal norm against which political behaviour would be judged. I am not denying the clumsiness and eclecticism that characterised many of Clinton's actions, but I still think that something positive was being established, the effects of which would circulate and be sanctioned sooner or later.

The shipping and shackling of al-Qaida fighters to Guantanamo in Cuba and the infringements of some civil liberties in the United States, and to a lesser extent in Europe, show us that this dream has been shattered.

Here lies the crisis, or – to put it in the context of our meeting this evening – here we witness the resignation of 'liberal imperialism'.

Liberal imperialism! An appellation, a system whose inner contradiction is *more* contradictory and explosive than ever before.

When observing the decision-making process in the West following September 11, especially through the dominant political discourse and ideological interpretations, I have the feeling that behind it all lies an implicit theory, a theory that separates the world into those who have established their nation-state – in particular its main function as a security provider – and all the others, 'us' in my case.

For those who did, the liberal agenda is still on the table, even if the near future threatens to be more restrictive and authoritarian. For those who did not, basic human rights promise to appear like a grand luxury.

It seems that all that is required today from non-Western countries is to prove to the West that they can secure local stability, and consequently secure stability for the West. Everything else can be postponed, for it is essentially submitted to that purpose.

Denouncing and protesting against this implicit theory and explicit practice is, of course, a healthy thing. But what should be terrifying to all of us is that the world is being split into two completely dissimilar parts: one of them might be going a bit more stategist, while the other might be going stateless, and I am afraid, sometimes consciously, proudly so.

As far as values are concerned, we could be facing a new kind of danger. One which is added to the economic and political split. If, previously, for all good or bad intentions, the tendency towards the depoliticisation of human affairs prevailed, now the tendency is unfortunately towards the dehumanisation of politics. This is the danger, or the new danger, which is added to the economic and political split. This is the main threat we are facing today.

War and Literature

Two years ago I asked a carpenter who had done a good job for a friend to come to my home and build a bookcase that would house the many volumes scattered on the floor and under my bed for lack of space. The carpenter was a young, jovial man who enjoyed chatting when taking a break and sipping my Lebanese-Turkish coffee. Coffee encourages conversation, and each time we sipped coffee together, we'd get to know a bit more about each other. He was from the former Yugoslavia; he had fled the war-torn country after having been a fighter. He was fed up with the war and his mother had helped him get out of the country. Now he made a living painting homes, but also building shelves. Building shelves always brought an uneasy feeling, for when he was a fighter he used to break the shelves of the homes he and his fellow fighters occupied, burning the books.

'We were cold and we didn't give a damn about anything else,' he told me.

I too come from a country that has witnessed a civil war and I wouldn't be telling you anything new by declaring that wars create many casualties. Wars kill and amputate humans. This is a *vérité de la palice*. But there are other casualties: books stand first in line among them; novels that have turned literature into a tangible reality, a reality that transcends voice, space and time, a reality that can be shared by thousands, if not millions, of people.

I looked at my carpenter and saw many 'normal' young men I had known – our grocer's son, the brother of my hairdresser, the concierge of the building facing ours. They too fought, they too occupied and ravaged homes, they too burned shelves and the books that were kept in the homes they occupied when they were cold. The story of Bullet the fighter, the book-burner, became a play I wrote or, to be more accurate, a story that wrote itself and that I transcribed like an automatic writer.

November in Beirut – or is it Sarajevo? They have occupied the two-storey building at the end of the street. The people who lived in this stone house must have abandoned it hastily. You could still smell their presence inside, and see their faces in the pictures, hanging on the bedroom wall and in the corridors.

Bullet, the name given to him by his companions, glances rapidly and disappointedly at the bulky furniture made entirely of dark solid wood. He instinctively raises his right shoulder to release his machine gun and swears crudely: the way the owners had furnished their home bothers him ...

'Nothing but shelves and books, books and shelves on every wall, in every room of this damn place!' screams Bullet, who decides to light a fire, for it is cold and damp inside. (*There is no heating due to shortages of gas and electricity cuts during the war.*)

Sure, I was writing the story of my carpenter, and that of our grocer's son. But I was also creating a work of fiction, and fiction is half truth, half lies. It is part real and part imagination (imagination as in fear and as in wishful thoughts). When we outlive a war we cannot just rewrite it; we need to reinvent it and this is how I imagined Bullet.

As the broken shelves keep feeding the fire, a relaxed atmosphere engulfs the living room. (*For Bullet and his companions are tired after having turned all the furniture into logs to start the fire, feeding it with hundreds of volumes of books.*) Bullet, seated in the stubby and austere armchair, with his legs outstretched, reaches nonchalantly for the pile of books scattered on the floor. He throws them indolently, one at a time, into the glowing flames. The crackling fire becomes warmly reassuring, and soon all the others in the room quieten down as they listen to the appeasing murmur of the flames. (*No doubt the gentle face of my carpenter sipping his coffee had something to do with the way my story developed.*)

As Bullet is about to throw the small book he is holding he cannot help noticing the bright colours emerging from its cover. His hand is still, ready to repeat its routine, when he pulls it back towards him, his eyes marvelling at the intriguing images printed on its jacket. Now the book is closer to his face, a few inches away from the fatal flames. He unconsciously changes his position in his seat in order to better hold the book, gripping it with both hands.

What is the name of this tanned and innocent-looking young man sitting on the edge of the boat? The blue of his eyes is as sharp as that of the sea that extends to both sides of the cover. How can a man be so wrinkled? thinks Bullet, staring at the old man curled up at the other end of the boat. Both men are unaware of the threat coming from the depth of the sea, where a monstrous-looking fish is emerging. Can these two lonely men face such a ruthless attacker? This powerful and treacherous fish could easily overturn their flimsy boat. 'The Old Man and the Sea', says Bullet reading out loud the title of the small book. He then reads the name of the author: Ernest Hemingway.

Bullet in my work of fiction, Bullet the character I needed to imagine, is now under the spell of literature:

When all the Hemingway books he could find had been read

and reread he looked for new heroes, walked into their lives until he was totally involved with their fates. Bullet had no time left for fighting and killing, he was now travelling in wider worlds, deeply enjoying his solitude as his mind roamed across times and continents.

This is how I feel about literature; it should be the opposite of war and fighting. But am I deluding myself? Has literature ever been able to prevent wars? Were there not great poets, even novelists who liked war and promoted it? Is Kundera telling us something about war and literature when he speaks of *The Art of the Novel* as an art that comes with the rise of the individual in Europe? Isn't *Shehrazade*, a metaphor-opposing story telling of violence and death? So many questions that came to me through this poor Bullet of mine ...

The delusion that Bullet stopped fighting because he fell under the spell of the novel was shortlived. Bullet, in fact, never sat quietly on that armchair near the fire. He kept laughing loudly with his mates, kicking the shelves and thrusting the books without even noticing that each one was different from the other.

I can still hear the pages of Rabelais' *Gargantua* agonising in the flames. It took less than a minute for Homer's *Iliad* to be extinguished. *La femme du Boulanger*, Pagnol's tender little book, hardly resisted the killing fire. All the little Moliére plays, those little blue and white books that had brought humour into my adolescence, disappeared instantly. It hurts when I think of *Oliver Twist* being thrown to its death with total disdain. I cannot believe that *Les Miserables* was incinerated with such facility. Soon the fire grew so strong that even Averroës' treatises disappeared within seconds. Not one volume was spared: Darwin's *On the Origin of Species* followed *The Second Sex*.

A beautiful edition of the Bible was thrown with the *Good Soldier Schweik*; the *Communist Manifesto* was ignited at the same time as Joyce's *Ulysses*. I cry when I think of the rare edition of *The Thousand and one Nights* torn to feed the fire, its daring illustrations becoming a source of fun for these over-zealous lads. I cannot believe that these people whose faces are still watching from their hanging portraits had purchased Pavese's *The Moon and the Bonfire*, nor that they would have read Baldwin's *Giovanni's Room*. They were all extinguished; none could resist the hunger of the flames or the cruelty of their assassins. Tagore's *Poems* were suffocated in no less time than those of the famous Turkish poet Nazim Hikmat or of the prolific Arab poet al-Mutanabi. As far as Bullet and his companions were concerned, these volumes were made of paper, and paper was good for warming their feet. They were oblivious to their mutation into pages, into tales and stories.

(*The books selected are those my friends and I chose when confronted with the question: What book, among all others, would you save if you had to flee your home in a war situation?*)

Literature is inseparable today from the books that carry their stories. If we want to save literature we have to save the rectangular objects that carry and spread their words. We have to respect the book for what it is: an art object that we should defend, defend against censors, narrow-minded educators and, most of all, the dangers of war. Fiction has described wars better than any history book because a novelist, a true novelist, is not a warrior. Literature and war carry opposite genes.

Texterminators

Storyteller enters, attitude weary, inquisitive. Storyteller stands centre-stage right, opposite where the actors will enter.

Storyteller: It is a damp and windy night. November in Beirut. Or is it Sarajevo? They have occupied the two-storey building at the end of the street. The people who lived in this stone house must have abandoned it hastily. You can still smell their presence inside, and see their faces in the pictures, hanging on the bedroom wall and in the corridors.

Raquel enters.

Storyteller: Bullet. The name given to him by his companions, a name that suited him perfectly. He glances rapidly and disappointedly at the bulky furniture made entirely of dark solid wood. He instinctively raises his right shoulder to release his machine gun and swears crudely: the way the owners had furnished their home bothers him. It will be impossible to kick and push all this heavy carpentry out of his way.

Raquel. He needs a tough game and it always gives him and his companions great satisfaction breaking up the furniture of the houses they've 'requisitioned'. It is terribly humid and solemn in here.

Track 2: Pre-recorded sound of boots on wooden floor.

Raquel starts putting on a headdress. Music begins quietly, fading towards the end.

Track 3: K&D, 1 min 10 sec

Bullet and Anna, followed by Mai, enter dramatically, walking like men, gesturing with their shoulders. The three stand with their backs to the audience, facing the projected image on the backdrop.

Storyteller: It is cold and dark inside. Bullet decides to light a fire. The damned furniture is too heavy and he knows it would be hopeless to try to reduce it to firewood. Looking around, he realises with a triumphant smile that all he needs for his fire is available and in profusion: the house is full of books and shelves, the perfect material for starting a fire.

Projection switched off. Hands of three actors plastered on wall.

Storyteller: With the help of two other fighters, Bullet removes the carpet to make space for a safe fire in the middle of the living room. He shouts for more men to join them. Soon the dark room is bursting from its quiet emptiness and the house is rumbling with energetic male voices, their heavy laughter vibrating and merging noisily with their thundering (*next track starts here*) boots on the parquet floor.

Track 4: Underworld. 1 min 20 sec fading at end.

Hands moving nervously, steps, hands, neck and shoulders moving.

Storyteller: One tall, edgy young man is merrily throwing the books off one shelf; another, shorter and chubbier, is kicking them towards a rapidly rising pile; and all the others, including Bullet, are vigorously pulling the shelves away from the wall, holding them under their boots while they aggressively break them into firewood ready for burning. (*track 5 starts here*) The atmosphere in the room is electric, charged with the glitter of sweating male bodies. As soon as the first books catch fire, the reddened features of the invaders emerge triumphant.

Track 5: Underworld, 3 min 30 sec

Shaking, shimmying – only a few times – then Mai turns her back to the audience and does breakdancing-type movements, while Anna and Raquel interact in very broken body movements, ending in all three shaking. Raquel leaves before the other two, then Mai, finding a place among the audience, then Anna. Raquel puts on a white overall and rimmed NHS-style glasses and reads in a professorial tone from the centre of the stage.

Raquel: Violence is a common feature in most societies. Statistically, we know that it is predominantly a male characteristic, particularly amongst young men. There has been much controversy about the role of male hormones in aggression. Some argue that testosterone predisposes men to aggression. Overcrowding, temperature, noise and social pressures all affect the level in society. A young man's behaviour in a group may owe more to the effect of peer pressure than to his own experience. Philip Hawthorn rightly stated in the *Financial Times* that testosterone is more lethal than nuclear weapons. It should be banned.

Raquel leaves stage, removing her overall.

Track 6: 'Remembering' by A. Cohen. Music starts quietly. Next bit spoken over music.

Storyteller: As the broken shelves keep feeding the fire, a relaxed atmosphere engulfs the living room. Bullet, seated in the stubby and austere armchair, with his legs outstretched, reaches nonchalantly for the pile of books scattered on the floor. He throws them indolently, one at a time, into the glowing flames. The crackling fire becomes warmly reassuring, and soon all the others in the room quieten down as they listen to the appeasing murmur of the flames.

Remembering continues. As Bullet is about to throw the small book he is holding he cannot help noticing the bright colours emerging from its cover. His hand is still, ready to repeat its routine, when he pulls it back towards him, his eyes marvelling at the intriguing images printed on its jacket. Anna steps hesitantly onto the stage and moves to the centre. Her movements are in synch with the speech that follows.

Storyteller: Now the book is closer to his face, a few inches away from the fatal flames. He unconsciously changes his position in his seat in order to better hold the book, gripping it with both hands. What is the name of this tanned and innocent-looking young man sitting on the edge of the boat? The blue of his eyes is as sharp as that of the sea that extends to both sides of the cover. How can a man be so wrinkled, thinks Bullet, staring at the old man curled up at the other end of the boat. Both men are unaware of the threat coming from the depth of the sea, where a monstrous-looking fish is emerging. (*Anna freezes here, hunkered down*) Can these two lonely men face such a ruthless attacker? Their flimsy boat could easily be overturned by this powerful and treacherous fish.

Raquel (*walking on stage*): *The Old Man and the Sea*

Storyteller: ... Bullet reads. He then reads the name of the author.

Raquel: Ernest Hemingway.

Anna dances while moving away from centre stage, and freezes in a hunched position.

Storyteller: Bullet feels an urgent need to know more about the young man, the weak old boatman and their fate. He wishes he could travel on these same waters, sharing the endless space and facing the same dangers they may encounter on their way to the horizon. Bullet hesitantly opens the book and reads the first line of the first page.

Voice (*pre-recorded*): He was an old man who fishes alone in a skiff in the Gulf Stream and he had gone eighty-four days now without taking a fish. In the first forty days a boy had been with him.

Storyteller: When he turns to page two, he is already curled up in his armchair (*track 7 starts here*), his knees joining his bending torso and his head stretched towards the open book.

Track 7: Robeson. 2 min 20 sec

Anna dances to 'Sometimes I feel like a motherless child ...' and moves off stage towards end of track.

Storyteller: When, very late that night, he fell asleep, the room was silent and the fire dead, forgotten and unfed. He realised, frustrated, that he would not be able to finish reading his novel tonight. There was no light. He could have thrown a few more books into the fire and brought some warmth and light back into the room.

Instinctively, he tightened his grip around *The Old Man and the Sea* and held it against his chest.

Raquel: No, not this book! I want to read it all, find out who will win the battle, who will survive. My heart is aching for this desperate old man. I hope this Hemingway has written more novels. I want to read them all.

Music from Robeson continues a few seconds. Change of lighting. Lighter, day starting to break.

Storyteller: Early in the morning the following day, Bullet, fearing the loss of his newly discovered treasure, prevented his comrades from getting near the pile of books or the remaining bookshelves. And when darkness started to cast its shadow inside the house, and a bitter humid draught settled between its walls, the fighters decided to find a new location rather than argue with their mate. Bullet stayed behind and kept on reading. When all the Hemingway books he could find had been read and reread, he looked for new heroes, walked into their lives until he was totally involved with their fates. Bullet had no time left for fighting and killing; he was now travelling in wider worlds, deeply enjoying his solitude as his mind roamed across times and continents.

Mai (*screams from the audience*): This isn't the original scenario! Stop the show, this isn't right!

Simulation of power failure, lights go off. Actors run behind scene, creating feeling of confusion. Everybody quickly off stage. Lights on again. Storyteller back on stage, confusion, panic ... apologetic for mistake.

Storyteller: This is my story of Bullet and his encounter with books. This is not the story of Bullet and his companions. Things didn't happen like this in reality. I have invented *a posteriori* a wishful tale to please you and to console myself. The end of the story in the real world of these fighters is less, so much less, enchanting.

Raquel enters.

Storyteller: Bullet had never in his life attended school seriously. By the time he and his fellow fighters occupied the two-storey house, he had forgotten the shape of many letters, let alone the art of combining them. Why would he care about the fate of whole books? None of the precious books, accumulated lovingly, over many years by those whose pictures were still hanging on the walls had been saved during those damp and cold winter nights. They'd been consumed by the flames. They no longer existed. Bullet, in fact, never sat quietly on that armchair near the fire. He kept laughing loudly with his mates, kicking the shelves and thrusting the books, without even noticing that each one of them was different from the other. He was never excited by the colours on their covers. He had never felt the need to touch their spine and discover what they had to tell. He was oblivious to the secrets, the stories and the wonders they yearned to reveal.

Track 8:

Mai and Anna enter with a stack of paper, some of which they give to Patricia. Other actors and Storyteller start pulling papers and throwing them onto the floor. Crescendo and following Raquel's rhythm ...

Storyteller: I can still hear the pages of Rabelais' *Gargantua* agonising in the flames. It took less than a minute for Homer's *Iliad* to be extinguished. *La femme du Boulanger*, Pagnol's tender little book ,hardly resisted the killing fire. All the little Molière plays, those little blue and white books that had brought humour into my adolescence, disappeared instantaneously. It hurts to think of *Oliver Twist* being thrown to its death with total disdain. I cannot believe that *Les Miserables* was incinerated with such facility. Soon the fire grew so strong that even Averroës' *Treatises* disappeared within seconds. Not one volume was spared: Darwin's *The Origin of Species* followed *The*

Second Sex. A beautiful edition of the Bible was thrown with the *Good Soldier Schweik*, the *Communist Manifesto* was ignited at the same time as Joyce's *Ulysses.* I cry when I think of the rare edition of *The Thousand and One Nights* torn to feed the fire, its daring illustrations becoming a source of fun for these over-zealous lads. I cannot believe that these people whose faces are still watching from their hanging portraits had purchased Pavese's *The Moon and the Bonfire*, nor that they would have read Baldwin's *Giovanni's Room.* They were all extinguished; none could resist the hunger of the flames nor the impassible cruelty of their assassins. Tagore's *Poems* were suffocated in no less time than those of the prolific Arab poet al-Mutannabi. As far as Bullet and his companions were concerned, these volumes were made of paper, and paper is good for warming their feet. They were oblivious to their mutation into pages, into tales and stories.

End of angry scene. Raquel leaves stage, followed by Mai and Anna. Stage covered in sheets of paper.

Storyteller: I see a silent circle of dark ashes in the middle of the house. They are voiceless. Their stories and enchantment ... all dead.

Track 9:

Remembering again, voice of storyteller over the music ...

Storyteller (*quiet, resigned*): I know how you feel. I am still in shock too. I can still hear the sordid laugher of Bullet and his companions echo against the naked walls. The walls looked like gaping wounds after the shelves were torn down. They looked miserable without the infinite juxtaposition of spines that protected and comforted them. Before these terrible events occurred and turned their lives inside the house into a nightmare, the books didn't mind a little incursion into their stillness. On the contrary, when a hand takes a book from the shelf and exposes a little strip on the surface of the wall, they welcome light and fresh air. But now look at the state they are left in. Ugly, defamed and shattered. Yes, even the walls are crying for all those lost volumes, for the softness of their presence and for the comfort they gave those who visited the room they protected.

It's not the first time this kind of morbid gaiety had killed books. But Bullet couldn't feel anything towards these rectangular objects. If once, just once, somebody had whispered, 'Once upon a time ...' in a gentle soft way – the way words are uttered when we were children and vulnerable – maybe he would have realised that he was committing a terrible crime. Maybe he would have jumped out of his chair and saved some of them at least. If he had been given the chance to enjoy a moment of solitude with one of these soft rectangular objects, he would have shared our myth and he would have believed in the sanctity of words. He would have acknowledged their right to exist and say whatever they wished to say.

Maybe if Bullet had been capable of saying, 'There is a book that has changed my life,' or heard Italo Calvino's advice:

Track 10: voiceover

Papers quietly removed from stage at same time.

Voice: Relax. Concentrate. Dispel every other thought. Let the world around you fade. Best to close the door; the TV is always on in the next room. Tell the others right away, No, I don't want to watch TV! Raise your voice. They won't hear you otherwise. I am reading! I don't want to be disturbed ... I am beginning to read Italo Calvino's new novel! Or, if you prefer, don't say anything, just hope they'll leave you alone. Find the most comfortable position: seated, stretched out, curled up, or lying flat. Flat on your back, on your side, on your stomach. In an easy chair, on the sofa, in the rocker, the deck chair, on the hassock. In the hammock, if you have a hammock. On top of your bed, of course, or in the bed. You can even stand on your hands, head down in the yoga position. With the book upside down.

Storyteller: Maybe if Bullet had heard these words, my story about him in the two-storey house wouldn't have been a work of fiction.

Yes, if once, only once, he had heard Shehrazade's voice:

Dancer advances, movements deconstructing Arabic dance.

Voice: I heard oh happy King, that once there lived in the city of Baghdad a bachelor who worked as a porter. One day he was standing in the market, leaning on his basket, when a woman approached him. She wore a Mosul cloak, a silk veil, a fine kerchief embroidered with gold, and a pair of leggings tied with fluttering laces. When she lifted her veil she revealed a pair of beautiful dark eyes graced with long lashes and a tender expression ... Porter, she said, follow me ... The porter followed her until she came to a spacious courtyard facing a tall, stately mansion with a double door inlaid with ivory and shining gold ... The door was unlocked; the porter, looking to see who opened the door, saw a full-blossomed girl. She was all charm and beauty with a forehead like the new moon, eyes like those of a deer or wild heifer, eyebrows like the crescent in the month of Sha 'ban, cheeks like red anemones, mouth like the seal of Salomon, lips like red carnations, breasts like a pair of pomegranates. When the porter saw her, he lost his senses and his wits.

Storyteller: Maybe if Bullet had heard the tales of Shehrazade, he would have waited quietly for the voice of a new Shehrazade and her promise:
Voice: I am alive tomorrow night, I shall tell you something stranger and more amazing than this.

Storyteller: Maybe then he would have realised that telling stories, writing them as well as reading them, is a question of survival.

Maybe if Bullet had heard these words, my story about him in the two-storey house wouldn't have been a work of fiction.

Mai and Anna leave the stage. Raquel puts on white overalls and rimmed glasses and reads from centre stage.

Raquel: Men are nine times as likely as women to commit murder.

Men are ten times more likely to commit armed robbery.

Men are eight times more likely to vandalise.

Men are seven times more likely to commit arson.

According to Wrangham & Peterson, based on the statistics released by the FBI, altogether, American men are almost eight times as likely as women to commit violent crime.

Raquel takes off glasses and jacket.

Storyteller: I have to admit that I cannot explain why I'm not distressed in the same manner when I see somebody erasing a film from a videotape. But when I see somebody obliterating as much as a word on a printed page I go mad with anger. Sure, I protest when censors intervene and dig their scissors into celluloid, but I am devastated when I see a page torn away from a book.

Is it because of THE BOOK? Of God's words? Is it because of the authority of THE BOOK that one becomes appalled by any attempt to touch a book, any book?

Raquel (*with a threatening raised finger*): Don't mention the name of God! Don't you see what is happening around you? Watch out for blasphemy laws! Where the hell have you been?

Storyteller: Have we anthropomorphised these mute narrators to the point of confusing any attack on them with an act of rape? I do not know what the real reason is for our adoration for these exquisite objects, but one thing is clear to me: I may love what they are saying, or I may hate it, they may amuse me or annoy me, open new worlds to me, or take me back to where I feel secure; I will always stand ferociously against any attempt, well intentioned or not, to silence them.

Angry movements by Anna without music at corner of stage while Storyteller speaks.

Storyteller: Bullet is not the worst kind of book-killer. He didn't know any better. There are people who knowingly kill books. They burn them. They burn them because they believe that fire purifies. They want to purify the mind from their poison, from the knowledge they carry within – the kind of knowledge they disapprove of, or they dislike. Some book-killers want to suppress their own fantasies, their uncontrollable imagination. They want to fashion our life by destroying the lives they don't like and by printing the words that will firmly shape our destiny the way they see fit. The ugliest of these assassins came out one evening in Berlin, on 12 May 1939, to celebrate their biggest feast. That night they fed their roaming flames with thousands of volumes. Their victims knew no pity, their death was carried out in public. I wasn't there, but I still remember.

Anna leaves stage in resignation.

Storyteller: None of the book-killers hesitated on that evening in May, none of these hideous purifiers walked away during the ceremony, none of them did what the Bullet of my story did. They had electricity and they weren't cold; they burnt the books because they had one sacred and absolute message: words were not sacred to them.

Track 11: Indian music, voiceover music, 2 min 24 sec

Sandra enters and prepares for dance.

Storyteller: My friend Aamer loves books; he often talks about them. Last week he told me that in his country, when any written paper falls on the floor people treat it the way Christians treat bread dropped on the floor: they pick it up and kiss it. For this is the flesh of Christ. Likewise, in Aamer's tradition you may be hurting the gods if you tread on a sacred word. The name of Allah, or the name of Saraswati – the goddess of knowledge, music and the arts – is made of letters that should be worshipped, not fall underfoot. I have to admit that I have never kissed a piece of paper I have found lying on the floor after picking it up, but I sympathise with this tradition for at least one reason: it is better to kiss words than to ban them, break them or banish them.

Track 12: Dance Sandra – Saraswati. Indian classical dance.

All actors back on stage – in the middle on either side of storyteller.

Storyteller: I know, I am not naïve, and you are going to tell me that words and books can also be vicious, hateful and dangerous. Some of those who revere the Word have burnt words they did not like as well. I know that, and I sometimes hear myself screaming, 'How did they allow this to be printed on these pages?' Then I quieten down and tell myself that words have never killed anybody, they just tell you things. Their message is captured between the pages of a book, from where they cannot move. Words don't act. Humans act.

All together: Books don't kill. Humans kill.

On Being Undone

8 a.m. I refuse to open my eyes before catching the aroma of dark bitter Turkish coffee. I can't even start to appreciate this ambrosial beverage till I'm well into my third cup. The fourth and the fifth are sipped more slowly. My rushing around will start soon. But not yet. I'm still living horizontally and not ready to stand up.

Reading *Le Monde* in bed with my fourth and fifth cups is an addiction that I see no reason whatsoever to give up. Not all addictions are bad for your health. Nine AM. Finito, this life of luxury. It stops now.

Good Lord, it's almost 9.30! The rushing begins. The day is, has been, and will always be, a race against time. I used to be met by a huge pile of letters on my desk at work. They haven't diminished, in number or in size, but, while they lie on my desk waiting to be dealt with, there are now emails accumulating vertically on my computer screen.

It's 10.30 a.m. I have to finish this manuscript by 11; but that was 11 AM. yesterday. Oh, how did I forget! I have to call the council and the tree company because the tree in the garden is growing too fast, and something like three organisations have to be consulted before we can trim a few branches.

I read a bit more of my manuscript before confronting the tree bureaucrats.

We don't go out for lunch in London. There's no time. This is neither the Mediterranean nor a Mediterranean style of life. All has to be organised well in advance. This is why I'm always late: one spends two hours searching through a theatre magazine to select a play among the five-hundred-odd showing in London on one day, and they're almost all booked out! If one is to attend the opening of a friend's exhibition, one has to travel for at least an hour.

Will I make the exhibition of my friend today before the theatre? But how can I go to the theatre and finish the sculpture that is threatening to collapse if I don't fix more screws into its base? The screws – I need to go buy them from a specialist shop. Development means specialisation, and specialisation means I won't finish that manuscript today because the screw shop is the other side of London.

I jump on the bus. Only a crazy person would drive downtown. Last time I took my car downtown I saw an official parking sign that said: 'Don't even dream of parking here.' (Bureaucrats try to be creative sometimes.)

It's already 5 PM when the bus brings me back home. It's cold and it may rain; no chance of walking to the exhibition. I do, however, have time to go to the gym, though I can't afford to spend a full hour there. Forty-five minutes of exercise, rushing between the treadmill and the rowing machine. No weights. I hate them. Once I would have joined the dance class, but that was back in the good old days, when there was still enough time.

I arrive half an hour before the exhibition ends, feeling guilty because I'm late. I feel *so* guilty that I join my friend and a few others in the pub and miss the theatre. On the way home I realise the fridge is empty. No, we will not order pizzas again today! Noodles, then. I promise myself that tomorrow I'll cook.

The screws were not perfect, but I made them fit because I have no choice. I won't exchange them tomorrow because tomorrow I want to cook a real meal: this means that I have to do some grocery shopping. One cannot cook when there is nothing to cook with.

Ten-thirty PM. I listen to the news. Appalling, awful. Where is the world going? Still, the broadcaster tells us a beautiful story about a child who had been reunited with his parents, so we can go to bed feeling better. Thanks, broadcaster, for taking pity on us. Last coffee before sitting in bed. Sitting, not sleeping, because now the most important ritual takes place. Adjusting the pillows for the reader's dream position – two behind the back, one on each side – and turning off the big light once the reading lamp has been repositioned and switched on, I hold my book like a treasure trove, a life-saving tranquilliser. I'm travelling inside the homes and souls of the characters of the novel I began reading yesterday. I hold the book with warmth and pleasure. I only hear the voice of the narrator; the whole world is silent except for the voice of the narrator and his heroes. I reach deeper into their thoughts, grabbing the book tighter and pulling the duvet higher. I am being undone, I am not rushing, I am in bliss, I will read until as late as the night permits.

Also by Mai Ghoussoub

Leaving Beirut

Imagined Masculinities: Male Identity and Culture in the Modern Middle East (with Emma Sinclair-Webb)

Artists and Vitrines (with Shaheen Merali)

Divas (play)